# COM MACHETE

## VOLUME ONE

BY

FERNAN VARGAS

# COMBAT MACHETE VOLUME ONE
## BY
### Fernan Vargas

**With contributing authors**
**James Loriega and Joseph Truncale**

## PHOTO MODELS
**Manley Blackman, Mohammed Martinez, Quentin Batiste**
**George Tellez, Brian C. Johnson, Martina Muresan, Erin Blasier**

**COMBAT MACHETE VOLUME ONE**
**COPY RIGHT© 2020**

**First Printing 2020**
**Raven Tactical International**
**Chicago, Illinois USA**
**www.RavenTactical.com**
**www.TheRavenTribe.com**
**www.FernanVargas.com**

# THIS BOOK IS DEDICATED TO

## EDGARDO PEREZ & MIGUEL QUIJANO

## TWO GUARDIANS OF THE MACHETE TRADITIONS OF PUERTO RICO

# TABLE OF CONTENTS

| CHAPTER | PAGE |
|---|---|
| FOREWORD | 7 |
| INTRODUCTION | 9 |
| A BRIEF HISTORY OF THE MACHETE | 15 |
| SAFETY IN TRAINING | 23 |
| USE OF FORCE | 27 |
| NOMENCLATURE & TYPES OF THE MACHETEs | 33 |
| METHODS OF CARRY | 37 |
| BLADE GRIPS AND GRIP SWITCHES | 39 |
| GUARDS, HAND POSITIONS & MOVEMENT PATTERNS | 43 |
| FIGHTING POSTURES | 61 |
| FOOTWORK | 67 |
| DEFENSIVE TECHNIQUES | 77 |
| TRAJECTORIES & VITAL TEMPLATES | 95 |
| OFFENSIVE TECHNIQUES | 107 |
| OFFENSIVE COMBINATIONS | 135 |
| THE COUNTER THRUSTS | 141 |
| OBSTRUCTED ATTACK SOLUTIONS | 149 |
| COMBAT TECHNIQUES | 153 |
| MACHETE DRILLS | 159 |
| BLADE GRAPPLING | 169 |
| CONFLICT ANATOMY & PHYSIOLOGY | 175 |
| FIGHTING WISDOM | 183 |
| BIBLIOGRAPHY | 213 |
| ABOUT THE AUTHOR | 215 |

# FOREWORD

The martial arts has been strong part of my life, having begun my formal training at age 14. Now, over 40 years later, I have had the privilege of meeting and training with some extraordinary martial artist. Although I consider myself an extremely eclectic trainer, I'll use anything that works and I am notorious for adding new "twists" to my existing systems, but I'm still a traditionalist in the philosophical aspects of it. I'm old fashioned and believe that the martial arts should still be used as way of self-improvement, not just physically but mentally and psychologically as well. That being said, first and foremost is the students ability to defend him/herself by utilizing any means necessary to stay alive. In my opinion, as a veteran and retired police officer with over thirty years, I believe all training should consist of techniques followed by drills and then vetted by sparring. If it doesn't work and has no hope to, let it go...it really is that simple. Leave the "show" for entertainers, fighting is ugly and should be kept simple and direct.

Having thoroughly reviewed Combat Machete by Fernan Vargas, the book accomplishes everything that it was set out to do. Right off the bat, the reader understands that this book is Volume 1, and therefore a starting point with more to follow. The book manages to cover basics, history, nomenclature and techniques for the practitioner. The outline is easy to understand and will serve as a guideline for any student of a weapons based system of fighting.

The basic techniques covered can be added to any existing martial curriculum and will also serve as a starting point for those instructors wishing to improve their weapons training. I would strongly recommend that this book be added to your martial arts library and for the reader to read the book in its entirety, later it will serve as a continuous guide.

As with this book and all books of this nature, they are only guides that are designed to help you on your martial journey, it is not intended to replace a qualified instructor, so please, find someone who is willing train and work with you.

Be safe, train strong and make yourself hard to kill.

W. Cmdr. Edgardo Perez (ret.)
Maestro de Guazabara

# INTRODUCTION

# INTRODUCTION

I was 12 years old in the back of my grand father's house in Puerto Rico. He was showing me his fighting cocks but the only thing that interested me at that moment was the panga machete leaning against the side of the coup. It was love at first sight. I picked it up and felt a connection that only other blade aficionados can understand. My grandfather showed me that day how to cut cane. I love Bowies, Navajas, Kukris and a slew of other blades but to this day the panga is my absolute favorite blade.

Since that day over thirty years ago, I have created my own curriculum for the martial use of the machete. The system presented in this book does not come from any one established historical tradition. Our program is a distillation of blade tactics from Europe, North America, the Caribbean, and Asia, combined with ongoing common-sense research and development. I have had the honor of being trained and/or mentored by blade masters such as Joseph Truncale, Hanjiro Nii, Edgardo Perez, Miguel Quijano, Gus Michalik, Mr. Lopez, Gilberto Pauciullo, Peter Brusso, and David Seiwert. I hope to share the best tactics, techniques and insights that I gleaned from them.

The system is a blade system, not a disguised stick system. Although blade on blade fencing is used for reference and as a tool to build attributes, practical application will most likely be against dis-similar weapons. Our goal is to give the reader a complete, comprehensive yet simple method for the use of the Machete. Volume one will give the reader a good solid foundation. Future volumes will expand upon that foundation and bring the reader even more tools for the tool box.

## HOW SHOULD THESE BOOKS BE USED?

This series is primarily for the purpose of entertainment and information. There are those however who may wish to use it to train from. The series is not meant to be a training guide without the guidance of a qualified instructor. If anyone is interested in using the book as a training guide please contact me. I will connect you to a qualified instructor to guide you, or I will assist you myself.

## WHY THE MACHETE?

The Machete is the number one edged weapon in the world. While not as common in the USA, the Machete has a long history of use by all types of people, everywhere. As a weapon the Machete several advantages that can not be ignored.

### Stoping power

Machetes pack a wallop. Even a dull Machete can easily break bones and give you a really bad day. A larger blade translates to more effective slashes and thrusts which create more serious wounds than a smaller blade.

### Distance

Machetes offer a great advantage in terms of their ability to offer you distance from your assailant. Danger increases with proximity. The Machete allow you to fight from a distance, taking advantage of reach.

## Ammunition & Maintenance Free

Unlike firearms, Machetes will never run out of ammunition. The Machete needs to be sharpened and oiled every so often but otherwise it is a relatively hassle-free weapon which requires little upkeep.

## Psychologically Intimidating

I do not know of any human being walking the planet that would not consider a Machete a legitimate threat. Machetes are intimidating and everyone knows it. Machetes will give you a psychological advantage over your assailant.

## Inexpensive

A $5.00 to $20.00 investment will get you started with a Machete at any flea market or hardware store. You do not have to invest an entire pay check into quality hardware to arm yourself with an incredibly effective self defense tool. In the event that you need to ditch the weapon, throwing away $5.00 bucks won't break your heart.

## WHY ARE YOUR TERMS AND VOCABULARY NOT CONSISTENT THROUGH OUT THE SERIES?

The reason for this is simple. I learned different things from different sources. The terms I choose to use will explain where I learned the material without having to stop and explain every five minutes. I believe in giving credit where credit is due. Each concept and technique in this book will be attributed to its source by using the original terminology used when I learned it.

# A BRIEF HISTORY

## OF

## THE MACHETE

The Machete is a combination of a large blade, axe and a short sword and the practicality of this tool has made it popular all over the world. The term Machete comes from the Spanish language and the first part of the name (Macho) means male or strong and used to refer to sledgehammers. There are numerous variations of the same tool depending on the specific area or country. The Machete is popular all-over South America, and also in places like Guyana, Barbados Grenada, Jamaica, Tobago and other countries.

The Machete is often used to cut through thick brush as well as for doing various jobs in agricultural communities. The Machete is also used as a favorite weapon of many countries and has been used in numerous battles all over the world. It is a weapon used by many ethnic groups in West Africa. In the Philippines they also use a Machete like tool called a "bolo" which is employed for chopping through the jungle and for combat. The Filipino art of "Arnis" (Eskrima) is a fighting system which employees both the stick and the blade or short sword (Bolo) in their system

Another popular Machete is the "Kukri" which has a slightly curved blade which is used by the Nepalese. In fact, the Nepalese soldiers carry a Kukri Machete as part of their equipment. China also has a tool they use (DAO) for practical uses and for combat. In many countries the Machete is carried on their person and used for practical jobs and for combat and fighting. Even Russia has their version of the Machete called a "Taiga." In fact, they also have their armed services, including their Special Forces carry a Taiga. The Japanese "Wakizashi" which is a short sword is similar to a Machete in the length and having a sharp edge and an unsharpened side. Most of the techniques of using the "Wakizashi" are similar or the same as the Machete combat techniques.

Colombia is the largest exporter of Machetes in the world. Interestingly, there is even a country's flag (Angola) that shows a Machete as part of the design. The Bolo Machete and the Gerber Machete /saw combination are also popular in Latin and North America.

Throughout countries in Africa, Southeast Asia, Latin America and the Caribbean the Machete has been the weapon of choice of agricultural workers and guerilla fighters alike. Machetes have been used with great efficiency in rebel uprisings, revolts and guerilla actions in countries such as Brazil, Cuba, The Dominican Republic, the Philippines, and Kenya. In countries such as Rwanda and Haiti, the Machete has a much more sinister history, being closely associated with human rights violations and even attempts at genocide. The Machete also finds itself at the side of soldiers across the globe, as part of their general issue equipment.

In the larger cultural scope the Machete has a role in cultural identity of laborers around the world. In Brazil and islands in the Caribbean such as Cuba, Puerto Rico and Haiti the Machete has played a role in folkloric dance and games.

As a formal fighting art the Machete is taught in martial traditions such as, Mani, Capoeria, Kali, Silat, Guazabara, and Colombian esgrima de Machete. Similar weapons are taught in various forms of Kung Fu, Krabi Krabong and historical western fencing arts.

The Machete has also found its way into the hands of criminals. It is a signature weapon of MS-13 the notorious gang springing from El Salvador and is used by gangs and cartels throughout North and South America World wide crime statistics identify the Machete as the number one edged weapon used in assaults.

# A  BOLO MACHETE

# GERBER MACHETE/SAW COMBO

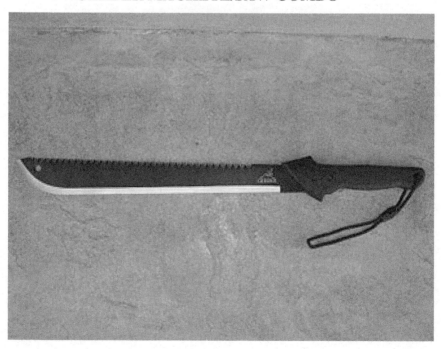

# U.S. MILITARY MACHETE HISTORY

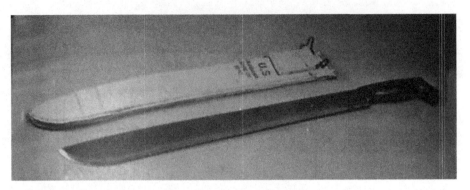

*M-1942 Machete and canvas duck sheath, with M1910 hook. World War II QMG photo.*

"Prior to World War II a 22-inch Machete was in use by the Army, but trials in Panama showed that a shorter design was better. The Machete adopted as the M-1942 was an 18-inch straight back modification of the Collins commercial type, proved by extensive use in the tropics."

This was the basic tool of jungle operations, permitting travel through the tangled vegetation away from the trails. The Machete depended on velocity rather than weight for its cutting action, being allowed to pivot in the hand with the stroke, while held only with the thumb, index and middle fingers. A hole was drilled in the handle for a wrist cord, which kept the Machete from being dropped or lost. The Machete was also considered a decidedly useful weapon, especially for the silent disposition of sentries and in night ambushes. (Photo to the left shows 101st airborne soldiers with a Nazi flag captured in a village assault near Utah Beach, St. Marcouf, France, 8 June 1944. Right paratrooper is holding a Machete that seems to have a bright finish.)

The sheath was made of heavy, water-repellent duck, which resisted the mildew and dampness that destroyed leather in the jungle. A brass top and staples prevented the sheath from being cut by the blade. A hook (M-1910 type) was provided to attach the Machete to a pack or to the pistol or cartridge belt. The Machete dimensions were about 22 1/2" overall with a 17 7/8" blade that was 2" wide.

Most World War II Machetes had black plastic grips, but True Temper Machetes stamped 1945 were made with olive green plastic handles. Other Machetes were made for the U.S. military in the World War II period. A U.S. Navy Mk1 model had a 26-inch blade and some of the older, 28 inch or longer Machetes remained in service. There was a paratrooper Machete with a 16-inch packetized blade, 22 inches overall. A folding Machete was also issued to some units.

The Machete itself has changed little since World War II, but the scabbard (or sheath) has evolved through several models. The earliest sheaths were a plain canvas stock with a belt loop. The M-1942 Machete had a sturdy canvas duck scabbard with the M-1910 belt hook. The last WW II model had a smooth, hard OD plastic case with a metal throat similar to a bayonet. That last style was in use until the Vietnam War, approximately 1966. In 1967 a new style carrier was issued that is very similar to today's Machete sheath.

The current version of the Machete sheath (photo, below) differs only in color from the Vietnam era M-1967 issue scabbard. The NSN has changed to 8465-00-926-4932 but the specification remains MIL-S-2329.

*"Sheath, Machete" (for 18-inch-long, 2-1/4-inch-wide blade) NSN: 8465-00-926-4932.*

# SAFETY IN TRAINING

## SAFETY IN TRAINING

Safety should be the paramount consideration during any training activity. We train so that we can protect ourselves and not get hurt. Why then would we allow being hurt in training? It is the responsibility of the instructor and all class participants to ensure the safety of all. All participants in a training activity should be led through a proper warm up and stretching routine before class begins.

## SAFETY EQUIPMENT

You should also use appropriate safety equipment for all training sessions. Equipment that should be used includes:

-Athletic Cup                    -Forearm shields

-Athletic Mouth Piece            -Safety Goggles

-Safety head gear                -Safety Gloves

## SAFETY TRAINING WEAPONS

You should also use safe training weapons. A variety of training blades, bludgeons and pistols should be used from rubber to aluminum trainers. NO LIVE WEAPONS SHOULD EVER BE ALLOWED IN THE TRAINING AREA. A good friend of mine was working in a seminar with another instructor. The Instructor drew his blade and cut my friend across the inside of his forearm as part of his demo. The only problem is that he drew his live blade and not a trainer. Luckily a few stitches were all that were needed that day. I shudder to think what would have happened if the instructor would have been demonstrating a neck cut?

## OTHER CONSIDERATIONS

- Training should be conducted in reasonable proximity of emergency medical care

- Training should be conducted in a designated training area with adequate flooring, padding and ventilation.

# USE OF FORCE

# SAMPLE FORCE CONTINUUM

| ASSAILANT'S ACTION | YOUR RESPONSE |
|---|---|
| Cooperation | Verbal Commands |
| Passive Resistance | Escort Control |
| Active Resistance | Control & Compliance Holds |
| Assault Which Can Result in Bodily Harm | Defensive Tactics/Mechanical Controls/Less Lethal Weapons |
| Assault Which Can Result In Serious Bodily Harm or Death | Deadly Force |

*The use of force continuum presented is a general model based on common U.S. use of force guidelines. The continuum presented is for illustrative purposes only. The reader is responsible for following all local, state and federal laws.*

# FORCE CONTINUUM

The force continuum is a conceptual tool which exists to aid in determining what level of force is required and justified in controlling the actions of an assailant. Verbal commands, escort techniques, mechanical controls, and deadly force are all options which are available to a person depending upon the assailant's actions. Force escalation must cease when the assailant complies with the commands of the practitioner, and/or the situation is controlled by the practitioner. The model presented bellow consists of five levels. Physical defensive tactics are appropriate from levels three to five.

**Level One:** The assailant cooperates with your verbal commands. Physical actions are not required.

**Level Two:** The assailant is unresponsive to verbal commands. Assailant cooperation however is achieved with escort techniques.

**Level Three:** The assailant actively resists your attempts to control without being assault. Compliance and control holds as well as pain compliance techniques are appropriate actions at this time.

**Level Four:** The assailant assaults you or another person with actions which are likely to cause bodily harm. Appropriate action would include mechanical controls or defensive tactics such as stunning techniques. Impact and chemical weapons may be appropriate at this level.

**Level Five:** The assailant assaults you or another person with actions which are likely to cause serious bodily harm or death if not stopped immediately. Appropriate action could include deadly force through mechanical controls, Impact weapons or firearms. Deadly force should be considered only when all avenues for escape have been exhausted, as well as when lesser means have been exhausted, are unavailable or cannot be reasonably employed.

## DECISION OF FORCE

When making the decision to use force you should use the minimal amount of "Reasonable" force necessary to safely control the situation at hand. When using deadly force for self defense you must be prepared to articulate and justify their use of a force.

"Reasonable force" can be defined: *force that is not excessive and is the least amount of force that will permit safe control of the situation while still maintaining a level of safety for himself or herself and the public.*

*You may be justified in the use of force when they* reasonably believe it to be necessary to defend yourself or another from bodily harm and have no avenue for reasonable escape.

Escalation and de-escalation of resistance and response may occur without going through each successive level. You have the option to escalate or disengage, repeat the technique, or escalate to any level at any time. However, you will need to justify any response to resistance.

## TOTALITY OF CIRCUMSTANCES

Totality of circumstances refers to all facts and circumstances known to you at the time. The totality of circumstances includes consideration of the assailant's form of resistance, all reasonably perceived factors that may have an effect on the situation, and the response options available to you.

## SAMPLE FACTORS MAY INCLUDE THE FOLLOWING:

- o  Severity of the assault or battery
- o  Assailant is an immediate threat
- o  Assailant's mental or psychiatric history, if known to you
- o  Assailant's violent history, if known to you
- o  Assailant's combative skills
- o  Assailant's access to weapons
- o  Innocent bystanders who could be harmed
- o  Number of assailant's you are facing
- o  Duration of confrontation
- o  Assailant's size, age, weight, and physical condition
- o  Your size, age, weight, physical condition, and defensive tactics expertise

o   Environmental factors, such as physical terrain, weather conditions, etc.

In all cases where your assessment and decision are questioned you may need to demonstrate the following:

o   That you felt physically threatened by and in danger from the suspect, i.e. that the suspect's behavior (body language/ words / actions) were aggressive and threatening;

o   That you used force as a last resort, and that you used the reasonable amount;

o   That you stopped using force once you had the suspect and the situation under control.

o   That you have exhausted all reasonable efforts to escape the situation.

# NOMENCLATURE
# &
# TYPES OF MACHETES

There are several different models of the Machete, but the basic nomenclature is the same on most of them. Besides the military type of Machetes there are also various Kukri types of Machetes which are also excellent for chopping brush and for self-defense.

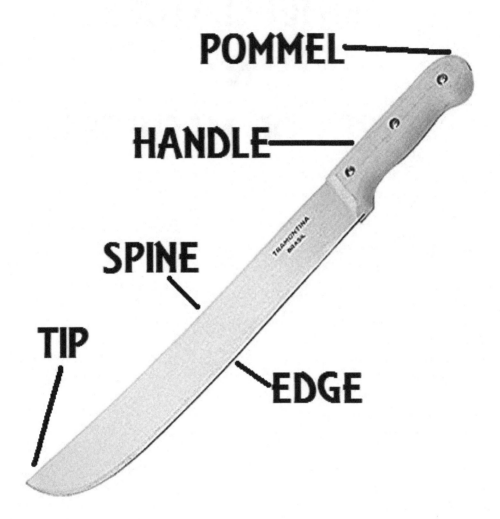

POMMEL

HANDLE

SPINE

TIP

EDGE

# TYPES OF MACHETES

## BARONG MACHETE

The Barong Machete is a traditional design from the Philippines. It is identified by its leaf shaped blade. The Barong is normally sharpened on only one side.

## BILLHOOK MACHETE

The billhook Machete has a curved blade and is sharpened on its inner curve.

## BOLO MACHETES

The Bolo Machete is a design commonly found in southeast Asia. The Bolo was famously used by troops on the battlefield. The Volo brigades used the Bolo to great success.

## LATIN MACHETE

The Latin style Machete is a common all-purpose Machete which is evenly balanced. As the name implies the design is commonly used in Latin America.

## CANE MACHETE

The Cane Machete is easily identified by its wide blade, small hook and the absence of a tip. The Cane Machete is used for hefty chopping chores. Wide, blunt-tipped Machetes perfect for hacking corn stalks and sugar cane.

## BOWIE MACHETE

A design based on the classic clip point knife of the American frontier.

## COLIMA MACHETE

The Colima Machete is weighted more on the front end and is one of few designs sharpened in both ends.

## HAWKSBILL MACHETES

The Hawksbill Machete is a curved tip design that is often sharpened on both sides. It is equally adept at cutting and thrusting.

## KUKRI

The Kukri is a Nepalese Machete which has gained much notoriety as the favorite edged weapon of the famous Ghurka regiments. It is a curved design capable of chopping and thrusting.

## GOLOK MACHETE

The Golok Machete is commonly found in south east Asia, specifically Indonesia. The blade has a scimitar like curve. This Machete is often taught in the martial art of Silat.

## PANGA MACHETES

The Panga Machete is most commonly found in the Caribbean and Africa. The blade is identified by a deep belly and turned up point. This Machete is often taught in the martial arts of the Caribbean.

# METHODS
# OF
# CARRY

There are many ways you can carry the Machete. It is important to note that the Machete may not be legal to carry even though it has legitimate and practical reasons why someone may be carrying a Machete on their person or in their vehicle.

You need to check with the specific laws in your area when it comes to carrying the Machete. Since many states may consider the Machete a blade like object and have restrictions as to blade length, you could be in trouble legally if you carry the Machete.

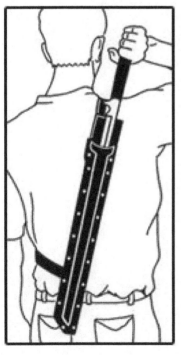

If you have a Machete you should also have a sheath for it. A variety of materials are available, from common cloth sheaths, to kaidex and leather.

A Machete is normally carried on the hip. This is the most accessible carry. The Machete can be worn on either side.

The Machete can also be worn on the back. Or in a back pack.

# BLADE GRIPS

# &

# GRIP SWITCHES

## THE FORWARD GRIP

The Forward grip is executed by taking the blade in the hand in a firm yet relaxed manner. The hand will form a fist around the blade handle with the thumb resting on the index finger. The edge of the Blade should be facing away from the Practitioner and in alignment with the Practitioner's middle knuckle line tip up to the sky.

Many instructors will advocate a modified version of this grip, often called a saber grip. In the saber grip the Practitioner's thumb will rest on the spine of the Blade. While this gives additional support through strong skeletal alignment, I do not recommend this grip. The reason being that a strong "blade beat", or even inadvertent jamming can easily dislodge the weapon. If this grip is used it should be done so sparingly once the Practitioner is in the midst of an attack. It should also be noted that the stripping defense methods found in south East Asian martial arts are often less effective against the Forward grip as opposed to the saber grip. The Forward grip should be used when maximum range is desired as it allows the Practitioner to more effectively work from the long range.

## GRIP CHANGE: PALMING

In the palming switch the blade will change hands but not orientation (heaven vs. earth). In order to use a Palming grip change the Practitioner will bring their blade to their center line. Once at center line the live hand will open and will meet the weapon hand, covering it. As this is occurring, the rear leg will step up to the same depth as the lead leg. At this point the Practitioner will pass the blade from one hand to the other. Once the blade has switched hands, the former lead leg will fall to the back so that the lead leg will match the blade hand.

# GUARDS, HAND POSITIONS

# &

# MOVEMENT PATTERNS

## HAND POSITIONING

Camillo Agrippa was an Italian Mathematician, engineer and architect who wrote Tratto Di Scienzia d'Armes, a Rapier fencing manual studied widely to this day. Agrippa was the first to present and breakdown the four hand positions used by almost every fencer since. The hand positions in fencing are directly related to the guards based on the quadrant concept. Each is used in conjunction with a guard in order to cover the four quadrants of the body. This is also the case in our system. While we use more guards than the classic four, our additional guards come only from how we choose to categorize the variations in elevation of the hand and are essentially the same as those taught by Agrippa. The four hand positions are: Prima (first), Seconda (second), Terz (third), Quarta (fourth). Larry Tom, in the article Hand Work for the Dueling Sword explains that;

*"The hand positions relate directly to the guards, each of which protects one of the four quadrants. Once you assume one of the guards, you have closed that quadrant off from your opponent's attack, leaving the other three quadrants vulnerable to an attack. Because you are aware that the guard in which you position yourself only protects you in that one quadrant, you are "inviting" your opponent to attack in one of the other quadrants. The key in the invitation is to anticipate and even direct your opponent's attack so that you in turn can successfully defend and counterattack. "*

## PRIMA

In Prima your palm will be facing to the outside and your thumb will be pointing downward on a vertical line. Prima is used to cover the low inside quadrant. The natural thrusting line for Prima is inward. The Prima hand position lends itself to overhead guards. Guards using Prima will offer excellent protection to the upper parts of the body.

## SECONDA

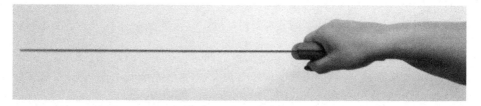

In Seconda your palm will be facing downwards to the floor and your thumb will be pointing to the left. Seconda is used to cover the low outside quadrant. The natural thrusting line for Seconda is from outside to inside. The Seconda hand position lends itself to outside guards. Seconda protects the upper body almost as well as Prima.

## TERZA

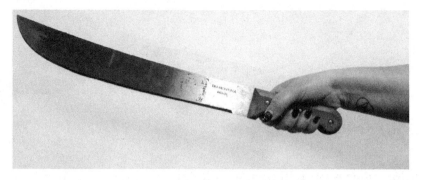

In Terza your palm will be facing left and your thumb will be pointing upwards on a vertical line. Terza is used to cover the high outside quadrant. The natural thrusting line for Terza is straight in. The Terza hand position lends itself to guards down the centerline of the body. This hand position is the most commonly used. Terza is used in the primary stance and guard of the system. Terza allows for easy transition to seconda and Quarta.

## QUARTA

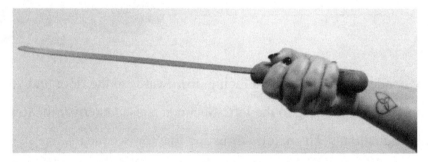

In Quarta your palm will be facing upwards and your thumb will be pointing to the right. Quarta is used to cover the high inside quadrant. The natural thrusting line for Quarta is inside to outside. The Quarta hand position lends itself to inside guards. Quarta is excellent for protecting the inside line of the body.

# THE NINE WARDS

In the Way of the Raven System there are several Guard positions that the Practitioner can assume. The primary default guard of the system is the center middle guard adopted from the "practitioner stance". This Primary guard offers good options to the Practitioner. From this guard the Practitioner has facility for both defense and attack. The eight secondary guards are postures which the Practitioner will find themselves in temporarily after an attack or defense motion. The Eight secondary guards can also be used by the seasoned Practitioner to invite certain attacks or responses from the assailant. An inside middle guard for example invites a high attack on the Practitioner's dominant side. The Practitioner can use this to their advantage. The Practitioner invites the attack by using a certain guard in order to pounce with a well-planned and timed counter attack.

Keep in mind that these wards may be adopted as initial postures or the Practitioner may find themselves in any given ward as a way adopting a defensive posture at any given point within a movement. For example, a Practitioner may execute a horizontal cut from right to left and find themselves in the "Inside Middle Guard" at the end of their action. A Practitioner may find themselves purposefully holding a guard for an extended period of time or they may hold it only briefly while in transition.

## CENTER HIGH GUARD

The Center high guard is achieved by holding the blade slightly overhead at the Practitioner's center line. The blade hand will extend outward away from the Practitioner approximately 12 inches. The hand will be in a thumb down position.

The point of the blade is facing the assailant. * In the reverse grip the hand will be held so that the bottom of the fist is facing the assailant.

## CENTER MIDDLE GUARD

The Center Middle Guard is achieved by holding the blade slightly above the naval at the Practitioner's center line. The point of the blade will be canted at a 45-degree angle towards the assailant. * In the reverse grip the hand will be held so that the bottom of the fist is facing the assailant and the forearm rests in a horizontal position.

## CENTER LOW GUARD

The Center Low Guard is achieved by holding the blade slightly underneath the naval at the Practitioner's center line. The point of the blade will be canted at a 45-degree angle towards the assailant. * In the reverse grip the hand will be held so that the bottom of the fist is facing the assailant and the forearm rests in a horizontal position.

## HIGH OUTSIDE GUARD

The high outside guard is achieved by holding the blade palm down in front of the Practitioner and to the outside of the body approximately 12 inches. The blade hand will be held the approximate elevation of the Practitioner's temple. The point of the blade is facing the assailant. * In the reverse grip the hand will be held so that the bottom of the fist is facing the assailant.

## MIDDLE OUTSIDE GUARD

The Middle outside guard is achieved by holding the blade palm down in front of the Practitioner and to the outside of the body approximately 12 inches. The blade hand will be held the approximate elevation of the Practitioner's diaphragm. The point of the blade is facing the assailant. * In the reverse grip the hand will be held so that the bottom of the fist is facing the assailant.

## LOW OUTSIDE GUARD

he low outside guard is achieved by holding the blade palm facing inside (thumb up) in front of the Practitioner and to the outside of the body approximately 12 inches. The blade hand will be held the approximate elevation of the

Practitioner's hip or waist. The point of the blade is facing the assailant.   * In the reverse grip the hand will be held so that the bottom of the fist is facing the assailant.

## HIGH INSIDE GUARD

The high inside guard is achieved by holding the blade palm up in front of the Practitioner and to the inside of the body approximately 12 inches. The blade hand will be held the approximate elevation of the Practitioner's temple. The point of the blade is facing the assailant.  * In the reverse grip the hand will be held so that the bottom of the fist is facing the assailant.

## MIDDLE INSIDE GUARD

The Middle inside guard is achieved by holding the blade palm up in front of the Practitioner and to the inside of the body approximately 12 inches from the center line. The blade hand will be held the approximate elevation of the Practitioner's diaphragm. The point of the blade is facing the assailant. * In the reverse grip the hand will be held so that the bottom of the fist is facing the assailant.

## LOW INSIDE GUARD

The low inside guard is achieved by holding the blade palm up in front of the Practitioner and to the inside of the body approximately 12 inches. The blade hand will be held the approximate elevation of the Practitioner's hip or waist. The point of the blade is facing the assailant. * In the reverse grip the hand will be held so that the bottom of the fist is facing the assailant.

# MOVEMENT PATTERNS

In this Chapter we will take a look at how to keep the hand in motion and more importantly why. Movement of the blade hand is essential for two different reasons. The two most crucial being:

-Movement as a defense

-Movement as a mask.

## MOVEMENT AS A DEFENSE

In an encounter a blade hand that does not move is referred to as a dead hand. The dead hand stays stationary and is therefore an easier target for the assailant to attack. Regardless of the body movement or footwork used if the hand does not move then the defense is compromised. When the Practitioner keeps their hand moving they are minimizing the chances of it becoming an easily acquired target by the assailant. The movement patterns are also intricately tied to the "Attack by Invitation". The Practitioner can bait the assailant into an attack and by skillfully using the various movement patterns the Practitioner can successfully evade the invited attack and execute a counter attack.

## MOVEMENT AS A MASK

The eye is able to better detect an attack beginning from a static position. For this reason the Practitioner should constantly have their blade hand in motion. The movement of the blade hand prior to initiating an attack is crucial. The Practitioners attack should spring forth from a movement in order to camouflage the attack. The assailant's eye will be much slower to detect the attack, giving the Practitioner the advantage.

The Way of the Raven System has adopted several movement patterns to aid the development of the Practitioner's skill. The patterns presented here are the ones most commonly used within the system. It should be noted that although there are several variations listed here, the Practitioner can move their blade however they like. The Practitioner can move their blade in a circular fashion, linear or diagonal as long as they KEEP *THE BLADE HAND IN MOTION!* Now don't go and be silly and move your hand in only one motion perpetually. This will be an invitation to your assailant who will eventually time your movements and make a successful attack. Vary it up and keep them guessing.

# THE CRESCENT MOON PATTERN

To execute the Crescent Moon pattern the Practitioner will bring their blade to a high guard just above their forehead. The Crescent moon movement pattern is a half circle. The blade will travel in a 180-degree semi-circle in front of the Practitioner. From this position the Practitioner will move their blade in front of their body in a semi-circle traveling either clock wise or counter clockwise. The Practitioner will trace this pass back and forth as they wish. Note that when moving the blade the point of the blade should always be aimed at the assailant. As with all movement patterns the Crescent Moon can be used for attack or defense. The Practitioner can attack directly from any point along this path or the Practitioner can use the pattern to invite an attack and then counter attack.

# THE FULL MOON PATTERN

To execute the Full Moon pattern the Practitioner will bring their blade to a high guard just above their forehead. The full moon movement pattern is a full circle. The blade will travel in a 360-degree circle in front of the Practitioner. From this position the Practitioner will move their blade in front of their body in a full circle traveling either clock wise or counter clockwise. The Practitioner will trace this pass back and forth as they wish. Note that when moving the blade the point of the blade should always be aimed at the assailant. As with all movement patterns the Crescent Moon can be used for attack or defense. The Practitioner can attack directly from any point along this path or the Practitioner can use the pattern to invite an attack and then counter attack.

## THE CANYON PATTERN

The canyon technique is one of the corner stones of our method. The Canyon comes to us from the Mescalero tradition. In the Canyon technique the Practitioner will use a "U" shaped motion. The blade hand will travel from left to right and vice versa along this "U" shaped path. While executing the technique the Practitioner should be mindful not to raise the blade higher than the shoulder level. The movement is executed from the elbow and not the shoulder. Note that when moving the blade the point of the blade should always be aimed at the assailant. The Canyon is useful as a general pattern of movement, keeping the blade hand in motion and therefore adding to the Practitioner's defense. The Canyon is also invaluable as method of evasion and setting up a counter attack after baiting or receiving an attack to the blade hand.

# THE STEEL WHEEL MOVEMENT PATTERN

The Steel Wheel is a Defensive and Offensive technique originally developed by Kenpo Karate legend and Combatives pioneer Grand Master John McSweeney. The Technique was also promoted by American Combatives Founder John P. Karry. The Technique is executed by holding the blade in front of the body and cutting downwards. The Practitioner will continue their motion downward and through in a 360-degree circular motion. The arm is rotated at the shoulder and rather than move in a straight line, the blade hand will circle slightly to the inside of the body. The blade should remain in constant motion once the technique has been initiated. The Practitioner can accelerate or decelerate at will. The speed should be altered constantly in order to keep the assailant off guard. The wheel can be expanded or contracted at will by bending or extending the elbow. The Inheritor of the American Combatives System, Joe Green explained that the blade should be pointed towards the assailant at all times in a circular motion like a train wheel. The steel wheel in effect creates a moving steel wall of defense for the Practitioner. An assailant will find themselves reluctant to even attempt to penetrate this defense.

An attack sequence advocated by both McSweeney and John Karry is to begin the steel wheel. Once in motion the Practitioner will circle the arm and as is lines up with approximately the level of the Practitioner's eye the Practitioner will execute a forehand horizontal slash, followed by a back hand horizontal slash and then a thrust. All movements are done very rapidly and with maximum aggression.

# FIGHTING POSTURES

# THE PRACTITIONER STANCE

The practitioner stance is taken by standing square with the feet approximately 12 inches apart. The Practitioner will then take their non-dominant leg and slide it back about 10 inches. The dominant leg will have the foot planted firmly on the ground. The non-dominant leg will be planted on the ball of the foot. The knees should be slightly bent. The hips and shoulders should be in alignment. The torso will be upright, do not crouch. The blade hand will be held in front of the body at center line. The elbow should be bent with the tip of the blade facing the opponent. It is crucial when adopting this posture that the Practitioner keep their entire body behind their extended blade. No part of the body should be flush with the blade or in front of it. The extended blade should be thought of as a shield. If the assailant wishes to attack any part of the Practitioner's body they must first contend with the blade.

Much is made about blading the body for target denial. We feel this is a mistake in blade fighting. One of the key reasons a Practitioner would blade their body is to establish a structure that is bio-mechanically correct for executing blows and strikes. In blade fighting the blade does most of the work and we need not adopt a bladed stance in order to deliver effective blows. Also, it is important to note that a bladed body is much easier to flank than a body in the practitioner stance.

## THE COMMANDO STANCE

The Commando stance presented here is a slight variation of the stance taught throughout WWII by such combative luminaries as William Fairbairn and Rex Applegate. The stance varies from the original taught in WWII in two significant ways. First the lead arm is held vertically not horizontal. Man is a vertical animal. Eyes, throat, heart, etc basically run down the center line of the body. The vertical lead arm can help shield these targets better than if it is held horizontal. The second difference is that the blade is held in the reverse grip. The reverse grip is used for maximum weapon retention. A blade held in this fashion is much more difficult to grab or disarm. The blade itself is a barrier to a grabbing hand by the assailant. The posture is taken by blading the body at a 45-degree angle, the blade is held closely to the rear with the live hand in front guarding the body's center line in a vertical position. This stance is used only against unarmed enemies or as a baiting tactic. A Practitioner should never take this posture when facing another similarly armed assailant. There are several reasons for this. First, an unarmed assailant is likely to focus on immobilizing the Practitioner's blade. By keeping the blade to the rear, the Live Hand is able to act as an obstacle to this goal by striking, parrying, and redirecting the assailant. The second reason why this stance should be adopted only against unarmed enemies is that while the live hand can be very useful against an unarmed foe it is an easy target against a blade. When the Practitioner blades their body and keeps the live hand in front as a vertical shield, the Practitioner is properly preparing to deal with an empty hand assailant. The bladed body structure and live hand to the front give the Practitioner good bio-mechanical structure to deal with incoming blows. Against an edged weapon attack this structure would be more or a liability than an advantage.

## CLOSED GUARD

The closed guard is assumed when the practitioner has deemed it necessary to use force and defensive tactics. The practitioner will normally adopt the closed guard as a temporary guard after delivering a strike such as an angle one or angle three strike. This position is appropriate to adopt when the practitioner does not feel it is safe to return to the regular conflict stance after delivering a strike. The practitioner should assume a good defensive stance with feet shoulder width apart and kneed slightly bent. The practitioner will keep the free hand in front of the body in a vertical or diagonal position. The Machete should be held in the rear hand under the opposite arm pit. In this position the practitioner is in a good posture to deliver an angle two or angle four strike.

# KNEE STANCE

This stance is advocated for use when the Practitioner has been knocked down or has fallen and must defend themselves before being able to recover to a standing position. The weapon is held back so that the Practitioner can use the free hand to block or deflect blows and kicks.

# FOOTWORK

## ABOUT FOOTWORK

For the Practitioner, good footwork is paramount. There is arguably no aspect of the fighting arts more important than footwork. The Practitioner will be well served to develop through drill and practice, flowing and quick footwork. Precision however, is more important than speed. The footwork of the Practitioner must be precise in both offensive and defensive actions in order to ensure success. A Practitioner can use good footwork to help control the scenario and maintain an advantage. Lack of proper footwork will make victory nearly impossible for the Practitioner. Proper footwork however can help to offset other weaknesses in a Practitioner's repertoire.

In any encounter a Practitioner can use linear movement both forward and backwards, diagonal movement (45 degrees) forward or backwards, and horizontal movement from side to side. It is crucial that the Practitioner learn to move smoothly in every direction, both on the advance and the retreat.

Whenever the Practitioner initiates an attack they should initially seek to identify the angle which will offer least resistance to their attack. By capitalizing on the least defended angle the Practitioner improves their odds of successfully completing their attack. This means that the Practitioner should attack on an open line, or attack after proactively opening an assailant's line. When on the defensive, the Practitioner should seek to identify the angle which is absent of aggressive force, in doing so the Practitioner rather than clashing with the assailant will simply evade or escape.

**THE ADVANCE**

To Advance, refers to any time the Practitioner takes steps towards the Assailant. The goal of any Practitioner is to always attempt to establish proper distance from the assailant which places the Practitioner in a position of advantage. There are times in which advancing steps are necessary to accomplish this. A Practitioner may therefore advance to gain the proper range to complete an attack or to jam or pass an assailant

## THE RETIRE

To retire refers to any time the Practitioner takes steps away from the Assailant. The goal of any Practitioner is to always attempt to establish proper distance from the assailant which places the Practitioner in a position of advantage. There are times in which retreating steps are necessary to accomplish this. A Practitioner may therefore retire after making a successful attack in order to be at a safer distance.

## WARRIOR WALKING

Warrior walking is just what the name implies. It is walking, a natural foot over foot way of walking. Like most people in the martial arts I was first taught how to "Properly" move, step and slide, step and shuffle etc. It was not until I began learning the Apache blade traditions that I learned the value of just naturally walking. The Apache traditions advocated natural walking because it is faster, more fluid and more natural than a shuffle step. At first analysis I thought it was a flawed idea. Upon applying natural walking in practice and sparring my teachers lesson was confirmed. The Natural step allowed me to move with greater fluidity. In most martial arts the student relies on proper stance for defense and power generation. In order to be ready the student must maintain this stance even while in movement. To this end the martial artist must move in a certain way as to preserve their structure. In blade work the blade does a considerable amount of the work for the artist. The artist is therefore not tied to a particular structure in order to generate power. Because of this consideration the natural walking is permissible.

## FORWARD TRIANGLE

The Practitioner will use a triangular footwork pattern to move toward the subject and inside the weapon's arc of danger. The Practitioner begins by standing with the feet together on the tip of an imaginary triangle or the bottom of an imaginary "V".

## MOVING TO THE RIGHT

While picturing an assailant standing in front of the Practitioner he or she will take a moderate step forward on a 45-degree angle to the right with the right foot. The back or left foot will remain stationary or will shuffle forward slightly.

## MOVING TO THE LEFT

While picturing an assailant standing in front of the Practitioner he or she will take a moderate step forward on a 45-degree angle to the left with the left foot. The back or right foot will remain stationary or will shuffle forward slightly. This simple stepping pattern allows us to move off-line of the attack, inside the arc of danger while still allowing us to move into the assailant for follow-up control.

## REVERSE TRIANGLE: MONKEY EVASION

The reverse triangle is the reverse of the female triangle. In this pattern the Practitioner will move backwards on a 45-degree angle.

## MOVING TO THE RIGHT

While picturing an assailant standing in front of the Practitioner he or she will take a moderate step backwards on a 45-degree angle to the right with the right foot. The back or left foot will remain stationary or will shuffle forward slightly.

## MOVING TO THE LEFT

While picturing an assailant standing in front of the Practitioner he or she will take a moderate step backwards on a 45-degree angle to the left with the left foot. The back or right foot will remain stationary or will shuffle forward slightly.

## FORWARD PIVOT

The forward pivot is performed by turning on the ball of your lead foot while simultaneously swinging your rear leg behind you

## REAR PIVOT

The rear pivot is executed by turning on the ball of the rear foot while simultaneously swinging your lead leg to the back.

## LUNGE

In order to perform a correct lunge step the Practitioner should take a small step forward with the toes up. The lead leg will bend bringing the knee forward. The Practitioner should take care that the front knee be just above the front instep of the lead leg. Bending the knee further could take the Practitioner off balance, while too shallow a bend will cause the Practitioner to take an ineffective posture. The rear leg will be at full extension with the rear foot flat on the floor while the free hand swings to the rear for counter balance.

## LATERAL EVASION

The lateral evasion is performed by stepping quickly to the right or the left. If stepping right, step your right foot out first then bring your left over and assume a well-balanced posture. When stepping left, step your left foot out first and then bring your right over and assume a well-balanced posture.

# DEFENSIVE TECHNIQUES

## VOIDING THE BODY

*"I was an on duty EMT responding to a call. Everything seemed like a medical call when we came through the door but moments into our evaluation things went south. As I attempted to reach down for my blood pressure cuff the young man jumped up and grabbed a full-sized kitchen blade off the cluttered counter and swiped at my face. I jerked my head back, as the blade passed by my face, then I hollowed out at the core when the blade swept back across the path that would have been my gut. "*

*-Master Jesse Lawn*

This story was recounted to me during my research by American Ninjutsu Master Jesse Lawn. Master Lawn successfully used the defensive concept of voiding the body to protect himself against an emotionally disturbed patient who made serious efforts to kill him. Master Lawn's account clearly illustrates the "Sway" and "Deer" techniques as taught in the Way of the Raven System. Both techniques are based on instinctive body reaction; this is one of the reasons why they are so effective. They fine-tuned variations of a movement that the body wishes to do instinctively when in danger.

In the world of Warriors there is an old adage, "The best defense is not being there."

We hold this adage to be true and it is a corner stone of our defensive maneuvers and philosophy. While checking hands and blocking techniques are a necessary part of any Practitioner's repertoire, I would like to pay special attention to the art of voiding the body as a means of defense.

In this chapter we will be looking at the defensive concept of "Voiding the body". In the Way of the Raven System Voiding the body takes a more prevalent role in defense than blocking or checking. Voiding the body is simply explained as such. When the assailant attacks any part of the Practitioner's anatomy, the Practitioner will remove said target from area of attack, thus protecting it from harm. This is done in a number of ways. In his writings Fencing author Capo Ferro suggests that a good Practitioner will always follow up a parry or a voiding of the body with a counter attack.

## TO VOID OR TO CHECK, THAT IS THE QUESTION......

The majority of the blade work I see in other schools and through video media is extremely reliant on the use of the checking hand. There are various drills that are popular training tools. These drills make their practitioners very good at checking. The level of hand speed and coordination is greatly augmented by these drills. At first glance it seems like a pretty effective way of training. It was not until I began training in the European and American Arts that I began to truly see the use of footwork and body voids as a means of effective defense. One of my instructors, Guru Brandt Smith once told me not to be lazy. He explained to me that footwork and body voids were essential to my defense. It wasn't until I was able to properly use footwork and body voids that Guru Brandt introduced the checking hands. I also encountered similar thinking in the Apache tradition. Blocking was not frowned upon, but if you could defend with movement, you were expected to. Interestingly this concept is not limited to blade work. The famous Bare-knuckle Boxer Mendoza also advocated voiding the body over using parries. I reflect back on Guro Brandt telling me not to be lazy. Laziness? Yes, he was right. I see it all the time. You see, you can get away with using bad footwork or under developed footwork without too many negative consequences if you're able to use the checking hand to compensate. This is a real problem. I personally feel much more comfortable using movement to defend myself. In spite of my personal preference I see the need to train both aspects of defense. I therefore go on the record with this statement. If you are using the checking hand to compensate for your footwork/body movement you are training incorrectly. Instead you should be using your checking hands to complement your footwork/body movement. This implies that you have developed both skills to the correct level and use them at the appropriate time and under the appropriate circumstances. If I am fighting in an open parking lot then I should be using movement as my primary defense. If I take a good cut to the checking hand to the point that it is disabled, using it may be a moot point. I may have no choice but to use footwork. Similarly, what if I am in a narrow corridor, or between parked cars? What If I have taken a disabling cut to the leg(s)? Footwork may not be an option and I sure as hell better know how to use that checking hand.

**THE SWAY**

When an attack comes at a high line, the Practitioner simply throws their shoulders backwards taking the head outside the arc of danger. The Practitioner will pull their chin to their chest and bring their hands under their chin while shrugging the shoulders. This combination of movement offers the Practitioner the greatest amount of protection. By tucking the chin and shrugging the shoulders the Practitioner is "shielding the carotid arteries. Bringing in the hands close under the chin keeps the hands from remaining out in the open where they can easily be cut.

## DEER TECHNIQUE

When an attack comes at a low line, the Practitioner will hollow out their abdomen and throw their hips and buttocks backwards taking the torso outside the arc of danger. The Practitioner's back will curl like a letter "C" allowing the hands will to come forward as a counter balance, and possible attack. In both cases the hands come up as a counter balance and more importantly to protect the vital areas.

## REASSEMBLEMENT

The reassemblement is the action of withdrawing the lead leg to the rear either to or past the rear leg. The reassemblement is used as a defensive technique as it voids the leg from possible attack. The final posture of the movement closely resembles the "Deer" defensive technique.

## THE DUCK

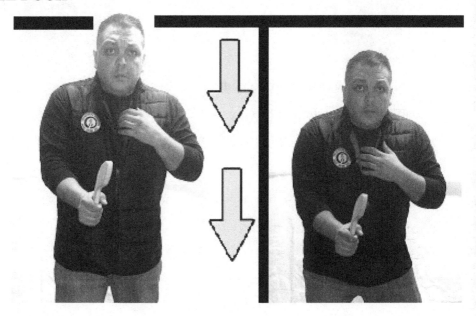

There are times when the best defense for a Practitioner is to drop their level in order to avoid an attack to the high line. To execute a duck the Practitioner must lower their level. This is achieved not by bending at the waist or lowering the head by bending the neck but by bending the legs while keeping the back and neck straight. This is done so that the Practitioner can keep their eyes on the assailant at all times.

## THE SLIP

The Slip is an evasive movement of the head used to avoid incoming linear attacks. Just as in boxing, the Practitioner will move their head and shoulders off line as to evade the attack. One trick taught to me by my boxing coach was to imagine throwing your shoulder at the incoming attack. This naturally creates the body mechanics needed to execute the movement correctly.

## VOIDING THE HAND

To defend both the blade hand and the live hand the Practitioner will "pull" the hand from the trajectory of the oncoming strike of the assailant. The Practitioner can use the hand movement patterns in order to achieve this.

## BLADE BLOCKING:

The practitioner has the option to block blade on blade or blade to flesh. If the Practitioner is to block blade on blade they should avoid blocking edge to edge. Blocking flat to edge or even spine to edge is a much more effective way of blocking as it is less likely to damage the Practitioner's blade.

When blocking into flesh the Practitioner's should push their blade out towards an attack and absorb the attack on their blade. The reason for using this method rather than cutting into an attack is that even if a Practitioner successfully cuts the attacking limb, the cut may be ineffective for several reasons.

Those reasons could include:

-Blade can not cut through heavy clothing

-Blade cuts attacking limb but cut fails to stop momentum of attack

-A Practitioner may be using an improvised weapon which has no edge

## HIGH BLOCK

A high block is executed against a vertical attack coming from high to low. Forcefully thrust your arms up at approximately a 45-degree angle from your body. The elbows are bent but there is enough muscular tension in the arms to absorb the impact and deter the attack.

## LOW BLOCK

The low block is executed against a vertical attack coming from low to high. Forcefully thrust your arms down at approximately a 45-degree angle from your body. The elbows are bent but there is enough muscular tension in the arms to absorb the impact and deter the attack.

## OUTSIDE BLOCK

The outside block is executed against a linear or circular attack coming toward the Practitioner. Forcefully thrust the forearm outwards towards the attack from the inside of the body to the outside of the body.

## INSIDE BLOCK

The inside block is executed against a linear or circular attack coming toward the Practitioner. Forcefully sweep the arm in front of the body from outside of the body to the inside of the body across the centerline.

## LOW INSIDE BLOCK

The low inside block is executed against a linear or circular attack coming toward the Practitioner. Forcefully sweep the arm in front of the body from outside of the body to the inside of the body across the centerline in a downward position. The elbows are bent but there is enough muscular tension in the arms to absorb the impact and deter the attack.

## LOW OUTSIDE BLOCK

The Low outside block is
executed against a linear or
circular attack coming
toward the Practitioner.
Thrust the forearm down and
outwards towards the attack
from the inside of the body
to the outside of the body.
The elbows are bent but

there is enough muscular tension in the arms to absorb the impact and
deter the attack

## ROOF BLOCK

There are two roof blocks that are used to cover the *right* and the *left*
side of the body and protecting the head and neck. They are so named
because the forearm and the blade form a frame similar to the roof of
a house. The blade is held at a right angle to the forearm, and the
gripping hand is raised above the head. The Blade's edge faces in the
blocking direction.

To execute the inside roof block the Practitioner will raise his weapon hand as if executing an empty hand upward block. The Practitioner's head will be in between their arm and their weapon which will be pointing tip down. The strike of the assailant will land on the Practitioner's weapon. The Practitioner should step on a 45-degree angle away from their weapon so that the assailant's strike glances instead of hitting with full force.

To execute the outside roof block (often called a ***wing block***) the Practitioner will raise his elbow so that their weapon hand goes to the rear and the weapons tip points downward. Some choose to rest the weapon onto the arm/shoulder closest to it. The Practitioner's arm and weapon should form the shape of an "A" on the outside of the Practitioner's body. The strike of the assailant will land on the Practitioner's weapon. The Practitioner should step on a 45-degree angle away from their weapon so that the assailant's strike glances instead of hitting with full force.

## SWEEPING CLOCK

To execute the sweeping block the Practitioner will drop the point of their weapon towards the floor from the outside of their body and then sweep across to the inside. This defense is used primarily against a foreword thrust to the midsection.

## LIVE HAND PARRY

The live hand is used to parry or redirect attacks. In order to use the live hand for defense the Practitioner will use an open hand to slap or push the oncoming attack of the assailant. A parrying motion should be short and crisp. A Practitioner should not over extend their body when executing the parry. The goal of the parry is not to be an obstacle to the assailant's attack but rather to deviate its trajectory away from its target by altering its course. The parry can be used effectively pushing an attack to the inside, to the outside, and downward.

# TRAJECTORIES
# &
# VITAL TEMPLATES

## ATTACK TRAJECTORIES

Thrusts or swings will be executed on particular lines of attack. All other attacks will come on one of the lines illustrated below. There are 9 attack trajectories, of which 5 are the primary work horse trajectories used for common defense. For this reason the majority of the striking techniques shown in this book are only used demonstrating the essential 8 trajectories. The reader however should know that there are additional trajectories that can be used.

# Fundamental Five Attack Trajectories

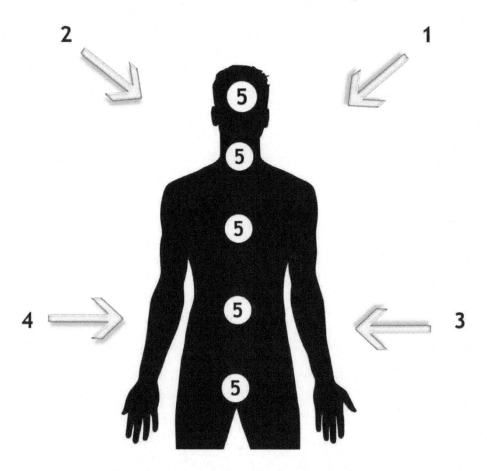

**Trajectory 1:**

Forehand downward diagonal


**Trajectory 2:**

Backhand downward diagonal


**Trajectory 3**:

Forehand horizontal swing


**Trajectory 4:**

Backhand horizontal swing


**Trajectory 5:**

A thrusting attack directed straight toward the Practitioner's front.
It can be delivered from any height.

# COMPLETE 9 ATTACK TRAJECTORIES

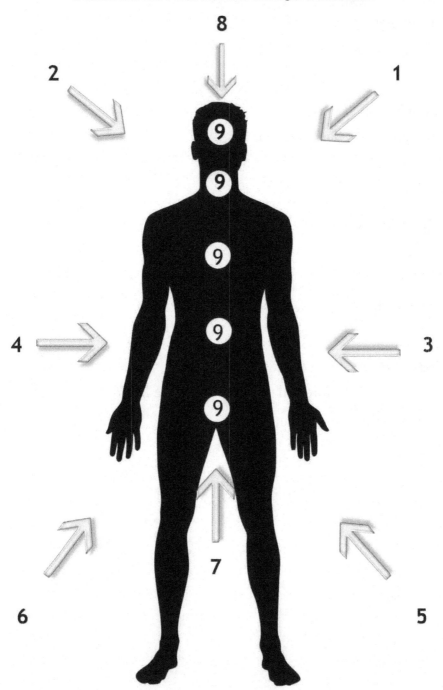

## The Nine Attack Trajectories

**Trajectory 1:**

Forehand downward diagonal

**Trajectory 2:**

Backhand downward diagonal

**Trajectory 3**:

Forehand horizontal swing

**Trajectory 4:**

Backhand horizontal swing

**Trajectory 5:**

Forehand Upward diagonal

**Trajectory 6:**

Backhand Upward diagonal

**Trajectory 7:**

Upward vertical

**Trajectory 8**

Downward vertical

**Trajectory 9:**

A jabbing, lunging, or punching attack directed straight towards the Practitioner's front. It can be delivered from any height.

## CUTTING & THRUST PATTERNS

In the art of the blade there is arguably nothing more important than understanding how to effectively move the blade in slash and thrust action. The attack trajectories as presented in the previous diagrams can be used as a pattern to teach students the correct lines of attack, fluid motion, and overall comfort in manipulating the blade. It will be useful to the Practitioner to learn and master the pattern. Various patterns are presented so that the Practitioner can break monotony in their training. The Practitioner should aim for thousands of repetitions with a focus on correct form while mastering the patterns. Speed and power will come as a result of having proper technique. As the old USMC adage states, "Slow is smooth, and smooth is fast".

The patterns should be drilled in the following variations:

## STATIC: STANDING

In the beginning of a Practitioner's training journey the Practitioner should practice each Cut & Thrust pattern form 1. Each stance, 2. Each ward, 3. Each Grip. When using the Cut & Thrust patterns in a static drill the Practitioner should stand in one place and execute each movement in the pattern selected. The Practitioner should begin slowly and then gradually increase their speed as their familiarity of the pattern increases. The Practitioner should also practice the Drills with both the left and right hand.

## STATIC: SECONDARY POSTURES

Once the standing static training has become comfortable the Practitioner should begin to adopt secondary postures from which to train the Cut & Thrust patterns. The Practitioner should use their imagination in deciding which posture to use.

I personally recommend at a minimum the following postures:

    a. On one knee

    b. On 2 knees

    c. Lying flat on the stomach

    d. Lying flat on the back

    e. Lying on the right side

    f. Lying on the left side

These secondary postures are important to train because unlike the Dojo, in real life a Practitioner may find themselves in one of these less favorable positions. The Practitioner Should make these postures part of their regular training routine. It is important for the Practitioner to become inoculated to these odd postures. The Practitioner should make every effort to instinctively function from these postures.

## DYNAMIC: ALTERNATING LEADS DRILL

Once the Practitioner has become comfortable with the Cut & Thrust patterns in a static setting the Practitioner can begin to incorporate movement of the feet and legs. One key drill is the "Alternating Leads" drill. In the Alternating Leads drill the Practitioner will choose a Cut & Thrust pattern and adopt a strong side lead. From this lead the Practitioner will execute the first movement in their chosen pattern. After the first movement the Practitioner will switch leads and execute the second movement in the pattern. The Practitioner will continue to alternate their leads for every movement in the pattern. By doing so, the Practitioner will begin to assimilate dual the dual motion of the hands and feet. In my opinion this drill alone can be worked at length to great results in the building of skill.

## DYNAMIC: WALK ABOUT DRILL

For the Walk About Drill the Practitioner should choose any of the Cut & Thrust Patterns and begin to simply walk forwards and backwards while executing the pattern. Footwork should be as natural as possible. Simple foot over foot as if you were walking to the park. The Practitioner should follow a training partner who will walk forward, backwards, and on off angles. This drill will allow the Practitioner to become comfortable with executing upper body movements while on the move. This drill is a natural progression from Alternating Leads drill.

## DYNAMIC: THE SPINNING MAN

For the Spinning Man Drill the Practitioner will walk naturally, following their training partner who will slowly spin 360 degrees as they move in order to give the Practitioner the opportunity to execute the cutting patterns and overlay them on a body that is in constant motion. The Practitioner will have the opportunity to work the cutting patterns on a moving body. This is important because most students will train the patterns while facing a target that is facing them. In combat an assailant may turn, and the Practitioner who has not seen this scenario in training may hesitate because they have not experienced this variation in the past.

## BLACK ARTS TEMPLATE

The Black Arts template comes to us from the Black Arts Military Combatives system of Grand Master Gus Michalik. The system and the template have its origins in the Canadian Military. The template presents us with a training progression for attacking various vital targets.

1. Forehand Slash to the left side of neck on a 45-degree angle downward, cutting the carotid artery.

2. Backhand slash to the femoral artery on the left leg, cutting on a slight angle upward from inside to outside.

3. Forehand slash to the femoral artery on the right leg, cutting on a slight angle upward inside to outside.

4. Backhand Slash to the right side of neck on a 45-degree angle downward, cutting the carotid artery.

5.  Stab to the sternum at a 45-degree angle upward, striking the heart.

6.  Thrust to the lung on the left side of the body, thrusting under the rib cage

7.  Thrust to the lung on the right side of the body, thrusting under the rib cage

8.  Thrust to the left side of the neck, twist the blade and in a circular motion draw the blade around the neck.

9.  Thrust to the right side of the neck, twist the blade and in a circular motion draw the blade around the neck.

10. Backhand slash your assailant across the throat making a horizontal cut.

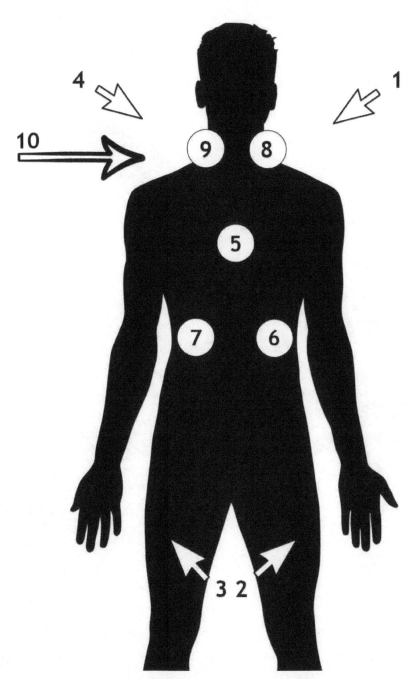

**Black Arts Template**

# OFFENSIVE TECHNIQUES

## TYPES OF ATTACKS

In employing the Machete, practitioners will use two primary types of attacks. The two are explained below.

## 1. FOLLOW THROUGH ATTACK

For this type of attack the practitioner should slash or thrust with the Machete at the desired target with the intention of completing the attack and following through in a committed fashion. This is the more powerful of the two types of attacks. The Follow through attack however has a slower recovery time than the Retracting attack.

## 2. RETRACTING ATTACK

For this type of attack the practitioner should slash or thrust with the Machete at the desired target with the intention of stopping at the desired target. Once contact has been made the practitioner will rapidly retract the Machete. This is the less powerful of the two types of attacks. The Retracting attack however has a much faster recovery time than the Follow through attack.

## OFFENSIVE TECHNIQUES

In this section we will examine the various offensive techniques used in the system. It is important to note that there are several variations of the techniques presented. Only the core techniques will be presented here.

## THE THRUST

In combat the thrust can be shallow or profound. The thrust is an attack that uses the point of the blade to penetrate into its target. To execute the thrust the attack should begin from the chosen guard and extend outwards towards the target for the thrust and then return to the chosen guard with the point of the blade oriented towards the assailant. A committed thrust should be made with complete follow through, bringing one's mass with them. When making a noncommitted thrust the Practitioner should move their blade out and back rapidly like a piston. In the Revere Grip the Thrust should be launched rapidly like a boxing jab. I have found that in the Reverse grip the thrust is much more effective than a cut at a distance. Thrusting from the reverse grip will help to offset some of the reach limitations found with the cut.

## ARM EXTENSION VS BODY EXTENSION

The thrust can be performed in two ways. The first is by simply extending the arm. The second is performed by extending the arm and expanding the body. This expansion is achieved by extending the blade arm forward while simultaneously pulling the live hand to the rear of the body. This motion will expand the Practitioner's chest. The motion is similar to drawing a bow and arrow.

## THE FOUR CARDINAL DIRECTIONS OF THE THRUST

There are four categories of thrust based on the area from which the attack originates and hand position.

The Imbroccata is a vertical descending thrust.

The Mandritta (Punta Mandritta) is a thrust coming from the outside of the body to the inside of the body.

The Roversa (Punta Roversa) is a thrust coming from the inside of the body to the outside of the body. The Stoccata is an ascending vertical thrust

In addition to categorization based on point of origin the thrust can be categorized by level of depth achieved in the execution of the attack. Shallow thrusts entering less than 2 inches are referred to as a piercing attack. Thrusts penetrating more than 2 inches into the target are referred to as stabbing attacks.

*In order to facilitate removal of the blade, and to create a larger wound channel, the Practitioner should turn his blade after a successful thrust in a "U" or comma shape before attempting to pull the blade back out.*

## THE ANGLE OF THE THRUST

Fencing master Puck Curtis in his article "Spanish Fencing notation Part 3: Fighting Distance" explains to us that Spanish fencing master Carranza in his work identifies the Right Angle as providing us with the best reach. If the hand is elevated, the angle becomes obtuse. If the hand is lowered the angle becomes Acute. Both the obtuse and acute angles have less reach than the right angle.

## THE LUNGE

To perform a lunge attack the Practitioner will extend the blade arm until it is slightly higher than the shoulder. The lead leg will bend bringing the knee forward. Ideally the Practitioner should have their front knee just above the instep of the leading foot. The rear leg will be at full extension with the rear foot flat on the floor while the free hand swings to the rear for counter balance.

# STANDING LUNGE

The standing lunge differs slightly from the traditional lunge. To execute the standing lunge the Practitioner must extend the blade arm and then shift their weight forward over the dominant leg while straightening the real leg. The movement is not as committed or dramatic as the traditional lunge. The Practitioner will find that their foot placement is not nearly as wide as in a standard lunge. *Note: the live hand is thrown back in the photos to illustrate the classic execution of the technique. In combat it is advised that the live hand be kept close to the chest.

# REAR LEG LUNGE OR REVERSE LUNGE

The rear leg lunge is virtually identical to a standard lunge with two exceptions. To execute the rear leg lunge the Practitioner will begin from guard position. The Practitioner will bring their lead leg back while extending their blade arm to attack. The Practitioner is in effect lunging on their non-dominant side. The Practitioner may also keep the live hand forward rather than backwards as in a traditional lunge.

# CUTTING TECHNIQUES

The cut is an attack that uses the edge of the weapon. In combat cuts can be shallow or profound. All cuts are made with a circular pattern as opposed to a straight line. The nature of circular momentum vs. linear momentum allows for faster flow from one attack to the next. Cutting in a circle rather than a straight line also helps the Blade to naturally return to the point of origin. When executing a cut the attack should begin from the chosen guard and extend outwards for the cut and then return to the chosen guard with the point of the Blade oriented towards the assailant. The smaller you make the circle, the faster you will make the cut. The larger the circle the more powerful the cut will be. For our purposes the cut can be divided into three categories regardless of the angle or target at which they are applied.

## THE SLASHING CUT

The slashing cut is delivered in a rapid manner. It accelerates towards the target, makes contact and is retracted all in one fluid motion.

## THE DRAW CUT

The draw cut is delivered in a rapid manner. It accelerates towards the target, makes contact and then lingers for a split second. Once the Blade has been placed on its target the Practitioner will then retract the blade with increased pressure drawing it back to guard. This cut occurs in two distinct motions. First placing the Blade and second, drawing it back. This type of cut is not as fast as the slashing cut but offers increased penetration.

## THE PRESSURE CUT

The pressure cut is the slowest of the three types of cuts but what it sacrifices in speed it makes up for in sheer power. A properly executed pressure cut can utterly destroy its target. The pressure draw cut is delivered with the same mechanics as a slashing cut or draw cut with one additional modification. In a pressure cut the Practitioner will use the free hand to reinforce the hand holding the blade. Together both hands will apply as much pressure as possible during the cut. This increased pressure guarantees an incredibly deep and penetrating wound.

# BASIC CUTS FROM THE FORWARD GRIP

## DIAGONAL FOREHAND CUT

To execute the forehand diagonal cut, the Practitioner raises the Blade to shoulder level and then swings downward on the diagonal line.

## DIAGONAL BACKHAND CUT

To execute the back hand diagonal cut, the Practitioner raises the Blade to shoulder level and then swings downward on the diagonal line.

## HORIZONTAL FOREHAND CUT

To execute the forehand horizontal cut, the Practitioner holds the Blade to their side and then swings horizontally across the body.

## HORIZONTAL BACKHAND CUT

To execute the backhand horizontal cut, the Practitioner holds the Blade to their inside and then swings horizontally across the body.

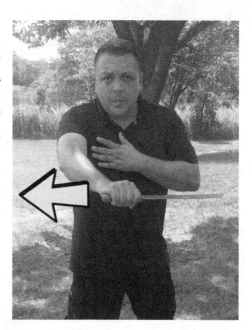

## UPWARD DIAGONAL FOREHAND CUT

To execute the forehand upward diagonal cut, the Practitioner drops the blade to their hip level and then swings upward on the diagonal line.

## UPWARD DIAGONAL BACKHAND CUT

To execute the forehand upward diagonal cut, the Practitioner drops the blade to their hip level and then swings upward on the diagonal line.

## DOWNWARD VERTICAL CUT

To execute the vertical cut, the Practitioner raises Blade to shoulder level and then swings downward on the vertical line.

## UPWARD VERTICAL CUT

To execute the vertical cut, the Practitioner drops the Blade to waist level and then swings upward on the vertical line.

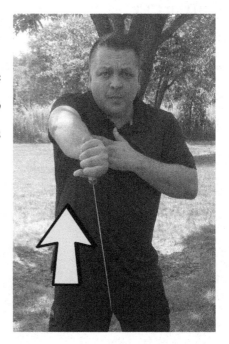

## DOWNWARD WIND

The downward wind is a cutting motion made by rotating the blade clockwise into a downward cut. The rotation is made from the elbow, not the shoulder. The downward wind is usually executed in twos. Like the "Steel Wheel" the downward wind can be used in rapid succession for defense. The extended blade should be thought of as a shield. If the assailant wishes to reach any part of the Practitioner's body they must first contend with the blade.

## UPWARD WIND

The upward wind is a cutting motion made by rotating the blade counter clockwise into an upward cut. The rotation is made from the elbow, not the shoulder. The downward wind is usually executed in twos. Like the "Steel Wheel" the downward wind can be used in rapid succession for defense. The extended blade should be thought of as a shield. If the assailant wishes to reach any part of the Practitioner's body they must first contend with the blade.

## BACK CUT

The back cut is a circular motion which utilized the false edge of the blade.  The Practitioner can utilize the back cut from the outside of the body to the inside or from the inside of the body to the outside.  The motion from either side is a swooping circular motion using the false edge or spine of the blade as the point of impact.  The inside to outside back cut is also extremely effective as a parrying motion.

# AXING

Axing is a fully committed power cut. The Practitioner will begin by stepping through with the strong side leg and simultaneously drop the blade from the high position down into their target. As the blade makes contact, the Practitioner will sink into a deep horse stance allowing their entire body weight to pull through in the attack. At the end of the attack the Practitioner will allow their attacking forearm to make contact with their thigh. This contact will prevent injury by preventing the Practitioner from cutting into their leg.

# SNAP CUT

The Snap cut attack is flexible and fluid attack that is executed with a whipping motion. The Practitioner will extend the blade hand out to the target and then retract it rapidly, in the same fashion that they would crack a whip. The attack can be made vertically, horizontal or diagonally. The Practitioner can use the spine of the blade, the flat of the blade or the edge. This attack is often criticized as not being a true cut. This is an accurate statement. It is not a true cut bound by proper cutting dynamics. I ask the reader however to imagine the amount of damage created by whipping a quarter pound of steel into an adversary. Not a cut or a thrust but a devastating maneuver none the less.

## THE STYERS CUT

CQC Legend John Styers taught the "vertical cut" in a manner that was very much unique to him and his writing. I will refer to this cut as the Styers cut and reprint the instructions in his own words from his book Cold Steel.

*"The thrust is the foundation of the cut. With the thrust you take your blade to the target. If a full thrust does not strike the target the natural whipping action will take place. This whip is the cut. The Vertical Cut is a thrust which ends abruptly with the thumb up, the nails to the left. When this thrusting cut goes straight to its target instead of ending in mid-air, this same whipping action will take place. The natural whipping action of the thrusting cut makes the blade drop. An extended extremity, such as a protruding arm, is an excellent target for the vertical cut. The vertical thrusting cut ends with the blade biting down, ripping forward, then snapping up again - all in a continuous action. Keep full thrust's distance from opponent's nearest extremity. If nearest target is hand or forearm, execute a thrusting cut. The blade is cocked in preparation for a wrist action to supplement the natural whip."*

# SAW

The saw is executed by placing the blade on the subject's body and firmly sawing back and forth. Like the hack, the saw is ideal for use in very close quarters because it can inflict damage to the assailant without great risk of the Practitioner injuring themselves. The Saw is best applied to boney areas of the body.

# HACK

The hack is delivered by using the blade to chop with. The hack is used primarily in very close quarters. The Practitioner will rapidly chop with the edge or the spine into boney targets. Like the Saw, the hack is ideal for  use in very close quarters because it can inflict damage to the assailant without great risk of the Practitioner injuring themselves. The hack is best applied to boney areas of the body.

# THE MOULINETTE

A moulinet can be performed when a practitioner extends their blade in attack and wish to make a second attack without retracting their blade. The practitioner can perform a vertical or horizontal cut from the wrist as a follow up attack.

# POMMEL STRIKE

Pommel Strike. The pommel strike is executed by striking with the bottom of the blade in a hammering motion.

## NATURAL BODY WEAPONS

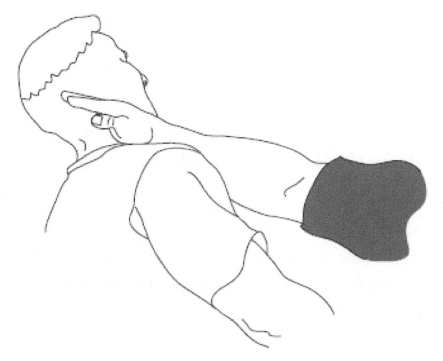

The Practitioner should not become fixated on their machete as the only weapon they have. If the opportunity presents its self, mechanical stunning techniques should also be used.

# FALSE ATTACK

A false attack is a feint. Capo Ferro calls feints "those deceitful gestures of the sword" It is an attack that is never concerned with actually making contact with the assailant. The false attack is used for several reasons which include:

-To read his response to certain attacks

-To gauge the assailant's attributes such as quickness or reach

-To lure the assailant by eliciting a certain response, such as drawing their guard away to which the Practitioner will have a planned attack.

–To disrupt the assailant's rhythm or momentum.

When executing a feint it is most common to feint in one direction and then attack the opposite. That is if the Practitioner feints high he will then attack low, if he feints left then he will attack right. This is not required but it is the most common way of utilizing the feint before an attack.

## MEYER'S DECEPTION

German combat master Joachim Meyer advocated a method of deceiving the assailant in his writings where the Practitioner would change cuts to thrusts and thrusts to cuts. In his works Meyer explains that the initial attack should be extended out towards the assailant half way and when the assailant begins to enact their defense, the Practitioner will change trajectory around the defense and change the nature of the attack from cut to thrust or from thrust to cut thus deceiving the assailant.

## STOP THRUST

The stop thrust is made as the assailant is preparing to attack. It is used to intercept the assailant's motion. The stop thrust must be well timed. The Practitioner must be able to anticipate or react quickly to the signs of motion that the assailant gives away. The stop thrust is exceptionally useful in stopping the assailant's forward momentum.

## RIPOSTE

A Riposte is a counter offensive action. A riposte is an attack that is delivered immediately after parrying an attack from the assailant. A riposte usually travels in the same line opened by the parry and is distinguished by the fact that the Practitioner does not re-set to their guard position after the parry and then initiate an attack, as that would be defined as a "*Reprise*". In traditional swordplay the parry which occurs prior to a counter attack is performed by making contact between the Practitioner's blade and the assailant's blade. In blade fighting, blade on blade contact may or may not be an option depending on the length of the blades in play. For our purposes a parry made with the body rather than the blade (such as the forearm) which is immediately followed by an attack is still considered a riposte.

## REPRISE

Unlike a *Riposte*, where a Practitioner returns an attack immediately following a parry, the reprise is a new attack that is launched after the Practitioner re-sets into a Guard position.

## REMISE

When a Practitioner makes an initial attack and then makes a secondary attack that follows the primary offensive maneuver without retracting their arm, it is referred to as a remise.

## THE REDOUBLE

Redoubling can be described as a renewed attack after an initial attack has been parried. If the assailant parries the Practitioner's attack and fails to riposte the Practitioner can now re-initiate their attack. The Practitioner's attack should be quick and occur before the assailant resets to a protective guard.

## BEATING THE BLADE

Beating the blade is an offensive action taken to clear a line for attack. This tactic is common in sword work. In sword work there is an intricate understanding of the best relationship between the Practitioner's blade and the assailant's. Focus is placed on proper positioning to gain leverage and angle. In blade work the tactic is much simpler in its application. To execute a blade beat the Practitioner will use the middle portion of their blade to strike their assailant's blade aside. Once the line is cleared the Practitioner will immediately follow up with their attack, usually a thrust. This tactic is perfectly functional with larger blades but is ill advised for small blades because the short nature of the blade makes the target area much smaller. This tactic is also very useful for disarming the assailant who adopts the saber grip. When I began training with the blade I was taught the saber grip. I felt comfortable with it until one of my instructors began knocking my blade out of my hand at will. He explained to me that this tactic was one of the reasons that he adopted a full hand grip and never used the saber grip. Since that day I have surprised dozens of training partners with the very same tactic.

# OFFENSIVE COMBINATIONS

## OFFENSIVE COMBINATIONS

When it comes to fighting combinations, I feel that they are best developed by each individual Practitioner once that Practitioner has found the best mix of their personal style, attributes and preferences. A few basic examples however are needed and useful to the newer student. Presented here is simply a sample of my personal preferred fighting combinations. Remember that with time each Practitioner should develop their own.

## SEQUENCE 1.

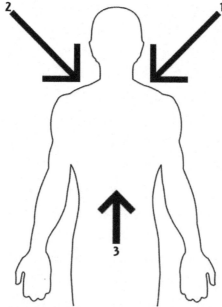

1. Downward diagonal forehand cut to the side of the neck
2. Downward diagonal backhand cut to the opposite side of the neck
3. Forward thrust to the heart (under the rib cage)

## BLADE SEQUENCE 2.

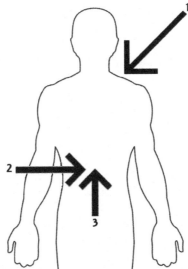

1. Downward diagonal forehand cut to the side of the neck
2. Backhand horizontal cut to the abdomen.
3. Forward thrust to the heart (under the rib cage)

## BLADE SEQUENCE 3.

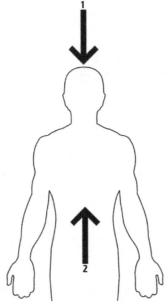

1. Downward vertical cut to the head.
2. Forward thrust to the heart (under the rib cage)

**BLADE SEQUENCE 4.**

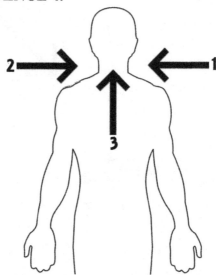

1. Forehand horizontal cut to the neck
2. Backhand horizontal cut to the neck
3. Forward thrust to the throat

**BLADE SEQUENCE 5.**

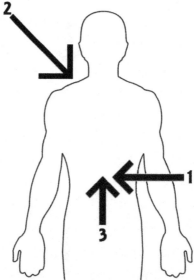

1. Forehand horizontal cut to the abdomen
2. Backhand diagonal cut to the side of the neck
3. Forward thrust to the heart (under the rib cage)

## ADDITIONAL COMBINATIONS

1.Snap cut to the hand, upon retraction of the hand immediately flow into a downward wind to the arm. At the end of the downward wind's circle immediately execute a thrust to the high line (Head Targets).

2. Execute a downward wind the hand/wrist area, immediately after the downward wind, execute and upward wind to the same target. Once you have completed the upward wind execute a back hand horizontal cut to the outside of the assailant's leg. Follow up with a thrust to the abdomen.

3. Execute a backhand horizontal slash to the assailant's hand followed immediately in one motion a backhand downward diagonal slash to the assailant's neck.

4. Execute a rapid back hand snap cut to the assailant's hand followed immediately by a back-hand snap cut to the assailant's face.

5. Execute a rapid back hand snap cut to the assailant's face. When they rock back immediately drop your level and execute a back-hand slash to the assailant's lead leg.

6. Execute a back-hand slash to the assailant's hand followed immediately by a thrust to the assailant's neck.

# THE COUNTER THRUSTS

## THE COUNTER THRUSTS

In this section we will examine the Counter Thrust Series. Presented here are 5 primary techniques and several variations; the Inquartata, the Stocatta, the Imbrocatta, the Passata Soto and the Torero. These techniques are presented here as counterattacks but with proper timing and presence they can be adapted to varying degree as primary offensive tactics as well. The techniques in the series come from a long tradition of European Blade work. There is much debate about the place of "fencing techniques" is blade fighting. Some experts frown on their use as impractical for blade combat. It should be noted that these techniques work much better with large blades than small ones. I however learned their use and application with a blade of modest size and have yet to find weakness in them when applied correctly. My friend and Western Martial Arts Instructor Keith Jennings once said ***"Using an Inquartata with a blade against someone who doesn't know what coming works is so well it's almost like cheating."*** I agree with Mr. Jennings whole heartedly. Over the years I have trained various people of instructor rank in their perspective blade systems. The introduction of this series of techniques has always been a "game changer". After brief instruction of these techniques I have seen these instructors sparring game grow and take on new depth. My good friend the "Hungarian Gypsy", John Kovacs is a trained saber fencer who learned under a former Olympic Saber coach. John has proven this point time and time again, humbling some of the "best" instructors of Asian blade systems out there in friendly competition. If you ask John what his secret is he will be happy to tell you that his secret is this set of techniques.

## IN-QUARTATA OR OUT-OF-LINE

The In-Quartata is a primary counter thrust movement. The In Quartata comes to us from the western fencing tradition and has been successfully adapted to large blade fighting tactics over the years. USMC trainer Col. Dexel and Biddle are two legendary combatives trainers who saw the value in adopting the technique to the training of their war time troops. The In Quartata is a tactic where the practitioner will bring their body out of line while simultaneously counter attacking. We will look at three distinct variations of the In-Quartata. The Practitioner will perform the action by stepping the non-dominant foot to the rear and past the dominant foot making a quarter turn. As the Practitioner's body comes out of line, the Practitioner will extend a thrust towards the assailant. The Practitioner can accomplish this quarter turn by either completing a compass step or a rear cross step.

## VARIATION ONE

In the first variation the Practitioners body will be taken out of line by sliding their rear leg behind and in line with their front leg. As the Practitioner's body comes out of line, the Practitioner will extend a thrust towards the assailant. The live hand is thrown to the rear as a counter balance.

## VARIATION TWO

In the second variation the Practitioners body will be taken out of line by sliding their rear leg behind and past the dominant foot making a quarter turn. As the Practitioner's body comes out of line, the Practitioner will extend a thrust towards the assailant.

## VARIATION THREE

In the third variation the Practitioners body will be taken out of line by taking a rear cross step behind and past the dominant foot making a quarter turn. As the Practitioner's body comes out of line, the Practitioner will extend a thrust towards the assailant.

## STOCCATA

The Stoccata is a thrusting technique that comes from under the emery's hand or weapon. To execute to stoccata as a counter thrust the Practitioner will step forward at a 45-degree angle using the female triangle footwork and thrust the blade from a low position upwards towards the assailant.

## STOCCATA DIRETTA

Step forward at a 45-degree angle using the female triangle footwork and thrust the blade directly at the assailant.

## STOCCATA ASCENDENTE

Step forward at a 45-degree angle using the female triangle footwork and thrust the blade from a low position upwards towards the assailant.

## IMBROCCATA

The Imbroccata is a thrusting technique that comes from over the emery's hand or weapon. To execute to imbroccata as a counter thrust the Practitioner will step forward at a 45-degree angle using the female triangle footwork and thrust the blade from a high position downwards towards the assailant.

Step forward at a 45-degree angle using the female triangle footwork and thrust the blade from a high position downwards towards the assailant.

## THE PASSATA SOTTO

The passata sotto is a committed attack to the assailant's low line. The Passata Sotto can be an offensive technique or used as a counter to a high line attack. Due to the committed nature of the attack it can be very dangerous for the person performing the attack. The Passata Sotto should only be attempted by a Practitioner who has developed an advanced sense of timing and distance. The attack in general is powerful in its ability to end an engagement but does leave the Practitioner in a position of vulnerability if the attack is not completed or is defended successfully by the assailant.

## VARIATION ONE

In the first variation, the Practitioner will take a very deep lunge forward. The left hand will post on the ground for balance as the

Practitioner executes a thrust upwards into the assailant. The Practitioner can also pivot to the right on the lead leg and shift the right leg to their right. The Practitioner will thrust with their right hand and drop the left hand to the ground for support.

## VARIATION TWO

In the second variation, the Practitioner will drop to their left knee with the right leg forward and thrust upward into the assailant's groin or lower abdomen. The left hand will post on the floor to aid in balance.

## VARIATION THREE

In the third variation, the Practitioner will lower their level by taking a very deep rear cross step. As the Practitioner lowers their level they can attack with a slash or thrust.

# EL TORERO

The Torero counter is named so because of the similar body posture adopted by the Spanish toreros in the bull fighting rings of Spain. The Torero combines the "Deer" defensive maneuver with a forward counter thrust to the assailant who is attacking the Practitioner's midline. As the assailant commits to their cut or thrust to the Practitioner's midline, the Practitioner will Deer back, voiding their midsection from the danger of the attack. Simultaneously, the Practitioner will thrust to the Assailant's high line which should be relatively well exposed. Targets of choice may be the eyes or the throat.

# OBSTRUCTED ATTACK

# SOLUTIONS

## OBSTRUCTED ATTACK SOLUTIONS

Guru Brandt Smith once told me that Blade Combat was easy. "Your objective is easy, Take the blade and put the pointy end into the bad guy. What he does in efforts to stop you is where things become more complicated." Truer words were never spoken. Unless the assailant has a death wish, he will take none too kindly to you impaling him on your blade. There will be times when the Practitioner is attempting to complete, and attack and the subject creates an obstruction to this attack. The assailant will do his best to prevent that by either grabbing your weapon (which will be looked at in a later chapter) or attempting to block it. The Practitioner has several ways to properly address the obstructed attack. They include:

## PULLING THE OBSTRUCTING LIMB

If the assailant has made contact with the Practitioner's blade hand in an attempt to block the Practitioner has the option of using the live hand to grab the assailant's arm and pull it away. The Practitioner should pull with force in order to disrupt the assailant's equilibrium. The act of pulling the assailant either downwards or to the side has the benefit of accelerating the assailant into the Practitioner's counter attack.

## PUSHING THE OBSTRUCTED LIMB

If the assailant has made contact with the Practitioner's blade hand in an attempt to block the Practitioner has the option of using the live hand to push the assailant's arm away, or forcefully smother it into the assailant's own body. The Practitioner should push with force in order to disrupt the assailant's equilibrium. The act of pushing the assailant can leave the assailant off balance and thus more vulnerable to Practitioner's counter attack

## TAKING A SECONDARY LINE OF ATTACK
If the assailant has made contact with the Practitioner's blade hand in an attempt to block the Practitioner has the option of taking the path of least resistance. In this scenario the Practitioner will simply adjust the trajectory of their attack and continue on to a new target.

# COMBAT TECHNIQUES

## THE BATTLE SETS

The Battle Sets are training routines. Presented here is the first of several in the system's curriculum. I am a fan of conceptual based training vs. technique-based training. I feel that when a Practitioner grasps a concept they will be able to apply that concept to create an infinite amount of techniques. I never understood why other instructors would teach techniques by rote. I always felt that it was so limiting to the student. I remember in the past I would teach a concept, explain it as thoroughly as I could and when it came time to apply it in training the students would hesitate and freeze. They seemed to have no ability to implement what I had just taught them. In the past I used to become frustrated with students and with my self as an instructor. Finally, I realized that some students are unable to initially think in such an abstract manner. I began to revisit the idea of teaching techniques by rote, not to give them just those techniques but more so to give them examples of the concepts at play. It worked wonderfully. The students were able to finally connect the dots mentally. After they became proficient in the "By the numbers" technique they were able to draw out the key concepts and apply them in a more conceptual manner as I had hoped for. Another benefit of set techniques that I discovered was that they were an excellent way of giving students a snap shot of a particular martial culture and philosophy. From this discovery were born the Battle Sets.

While the series offers the Practitioner reliable, functional answers to common problems their true value lies in their ability to train several skills simultaneously. While practicing the Sets the Practitioner will be training important skills such as target acquisition, correct posture, footwork, methods of attack and defense. The Practitioner will also improve their sense of timing and distance. While these sets represent techniques, they should not be considered dogma. Ideally, I would like to see every student learn the sets and then forget them. That is to say, I do not want them to become reliant on paint by numbers approach. I would be much happier seeing students learn the sets, perfect them, learn their lessons and intricacies and then use that knowledge to extrapolate and create their own "Techniques" that are unique to their reality, attributes and abilities. The only people who should be committing these sets to memory after they have been mastered are those who seek to instruct others.

## FOREHAND DIAGONAL SLASH DEFENSE

The assailant executes attacks with a forehand diagonal slash to the practitioner's head. The practitioner will execute an inside roof block. The practitioner will then simultaneously check the assailant's weapon hand while bringing their blade in a circle behind their head. As the blade comes around the practitioner will execute a forehand diagonal slash to the assailant's head.

## BACKHAND DIAGONAL SLASH DEFENSE

The assailant executed a backhand diagonal slash to the head. The practitioner will chop down onto the arm. Once the weapon is cleared the Practitioner will step in and check the assailant's arm simultaneously. Once in range the Practitioner will forcefully chop down into the neck/head region of the assailant.

## BACKHAND HORIZONTAL SLASH DEFENSE

The assailant executed a backhand diagonal slash to the abdomen. The practitioner executes a low downward block. The Practitioner will then step in and check the assailant's arm simultaneously. Once in range the Practitioner will forcefully chop down into the neck/head region of the assailant.

## FOREHAND HORIZONTAL SLASH DEFENSE

The assailant executes a forehand horizontal slash to the abdomen. The Practitioner steps forward at a 45-degree angle to the right and executes a downward sweeping block as the live hand travels under the Practitioner's forearm and grasps the assailant's wrist. The Practitioner will then immediately execute a horizontal cut across the assailant's neck.

## THRUST TO THE ABDOMEN DEFENSE

The assailant executes a thrust to the abdomen. The Practitioner steps forward at a 45-degree angle to the left and executes a downward block with the flat of their blade (edge facing to the left). The Practitioner will then make a small counter clockwise circle with the wrist so that the edge of their blade is facing the assailant. The Practitioner will then use the live hand to check the assailant's arm down as they advance, circle their blade and execute a cut across the back of the assailant's neck.

# MACHETE DRILLS

## WARM UP DRILLS:

Warm-Up drill: Your partner can use a training Machete or a stick to attack you with in this drill. Slowly your partner will perform a downward strike at your head, groin, left side and right side, as you perform each block using the training Machete. Do this same slow drill five to ten times.

## LEVEL ONE DRILL

As both you move around, your partner will make large moves to any of the four areas as you block the attacks. Do for one minute and change sides.

## LEVEL TWO DRILL

Back to a wall drill is done by the practitioner having his or her back to the wall where you cannot back up. Your partner will attack at all angles as you perform the four basic blocks. After one-minute change sides.

## LEVEL THREE DRILL

Begin slowly doing this drill. Both you and your partner can now move around again with one being the assailant and one the practitioner. The assailant can use any attack angle and the practitioner must ALWAYS follow the block with a counter-attack. After one-minute change sides.

''

## MEET THE FORCE DRILL SERIES

As the assailant Attacks the Practitioner, the Practitioner will meet the incoming attack with his weapon, coming to the inside of the opponent's arc of power. Meeting the force is most often a proactive way of addressing an incoming attack. The Practitioner must be aware that they use proper form, as the Practitioner is meeting oncoming force head on. Improper structure will buckle and give way to the assailant's attack.

## FOLLOW THE FORCE DRILL SERIES

As the assailant Attacks the Practitioner, the Practitioner is not prepared and is not quick enough to meet the incoming attack with his weapon, coming to the inside of the opponent's arc of power. The practitioner then uses body movement to avoid the attack and then address the attack on the "back end" by following the attack. Following the force is a most often a Reactive way of addressing an incoming attack.

## MEET THE FORCE/FOLLOW THE FORCE ADD ONS

Once the Practitioner has mastered these two basic drills the Practitioner can build upon them in the following ways. Once the Practitioner addresses the initial attack the Practitioner will adjust their position and then execute one of the following.

## DOWNWARD DIAGONAL CUTS

Once the Practitioner has addressed the initial attack, the Practitioner will execute forehand downward diagonal cut followed by a back hand downward diagonal cut.

## UPWARD DIAGONAL CUTS

Once the Practitioner has addressed the initial attack, the Practitioner will execute forehand upward diagonal cut followed by a back hand upward diagonal cut.

## HORIZONTAL CUTS

Once the Practitioner has addressed the initial attack, the Practitioner will execute forehand horizontal cut followed by a back hand horizontal cut.

## THRUSTING ATTACKS

Once the Practitioner has addressed the initial attack, the Practitioner will execute two thrusting attacks.

## THE CIRCLE OF DEATH

To perform this drill, multiple assailants will surround and circle the Practitioner. The assailants will take turns randomly attacking the Practitioner. The attacks will be staggered so the Practitioner can not time the attacks. This drill will assist the Practitioner in inoculating themselves to ambush or surprise attacks.

## 1-2-3 DRILL

The one 1-2-3 drill was taught to me by Reality Based Self Defense expert Jim Wagner. I learned this drill while taking Jim's Blade survival class in Buena Park California. I fell in love with the drill and I have found it to be indispensable in my training and teaching.

The drill begins with two partners, one defending and the other attacking. The assailant will make one attack and then freeze. The assailant will count a full three seconds before resetting. The assailant will feed the Practitioner all of the angles of attack in order and then randomly. In those three seconds the Practitioner can work any techniques that they like. Once this has been done a few times the team will switch to a two second count, and eventually a one second count. Now this drill has proven useful for a few reasons. First, the drill allows the Practitioner the opportunity to work their techniques against a variety of angles at progressively difficult time frames. Secondly, the drill is revealing. Students always work some really fancy crap when they have 3 seconds to work. By the time they get to one second they are working by necessity a much simpler and more direct skill set. Lastly the drill is an excellent way to prepare students for real time sparring. I personally do not like to let new students spar right off the bat. Newbies tend to get a little anxious or excited and they loose sight of sparring as a drill. The 1-2-3 drill allows them to work progressively towards real time sparring without neglecting the skill building along the way.

# BLADE GRAPPLING

## BLADE GRAPPLING

A practitioner may find themselves wrestling with an assailant. A grappling situation can be a difficult test in itself but can become the deadliest of encounters when steel is in play. It is best to avoid grappling against the blade. In the chaos of combat however it is inevitable that someone somewhere will be unlucky enough to have to face this situation. Times like those are the reason we train. Grappling with a blade is distinctly different from grappling without a blade. Whereas unarmed grapplers have the full use of their hands, Practitioners will be very concerned with using at least one of their hands to secure the assailant's weapon. This in itself is a game changer. What makes for good grappling changes when you take into account such considerations. The Practitioner will be well served to remember that while this is a limitation to themselves, it is also a serious limitation imposed on the assailant. A smart Practitioner, having trained in the way of blade grappling will be able to exploit this limitation. The three things that all grapplers learn are 1. Base, 2. Angle and 3. Leverage. One hand that is fully committed to holding onto the assailant's blade will seriously affect the assailant's ability to set a proper base or employ proper leverage. For this reason, it is arguably easier to grapple an assailant with a blade when you are unarmed rather than armed.

Here we will look at a series of scenarios and solutions to prepare the practitioner to solve this most dangerous riddle. Outlined below are common scenarios and their corresponding solutions.

## TWO HIGH-SEIZURE AND COUNTER SEIZURE

In this position the practitioner has attacked on the high line and the assailant has seized their wrist interrupting the practitioner's attack with their live hand. The Practitioner in turn has seized the assailant's wrist interrupting the assailant's attack. The practitioner and the assailant are in a stalemate.

## TWO HIGH TECHNIQUE NUMBER ONE

In this technique the practitioner will step into the assailant and throw a horizontal elbow strike with their blade side so that the elbow is positioned over the assailant's arm. The practitioner will then forcefully drop the elbow down freeing their blade hand and placing their blade in position for a thrust or cut to the assailant's neck.

## TWO HIGH TECHNIQUE NUMBER TWO

In the first technique the practitioner will push the assailant's blade backwards in an attempt to get the assailant to resist and push forward. When the practitioner feels the assailant pushing back the practitioner will quickly guide the assailant's blade to their opposite arm cutting down on the assailant's arm with their own blade. Once the blade has passed the assailant's arm the practitioner will violently lift the assailant's arm back up striking the assailant underneath their elbow. This blow will injure the assailant and free the practitioner's blade hand. Once the blade hand is free the practitioner can use their blade to attack the assailant

## TWO HIGH TECHNIQUE NUMBER THREE

In this technique the practitioner will push the assailant's blade backwards in an attempt to get the assailant to resist and push forward. When the practitioner feels the assailant pushing back and their arm is extended the practitioner will quickly use their own blade to cut down onto the assailant's extended arm. Once the blade has passed the assailant's arm the practitioner will continue their cut in a counter clockwise circle and bring their blade to the assailant's high line attacking the head or neck with a cut or thrust.

## TWO HIGH TECHNIQUE NUMBER FOUR

In this technique the practitioner will push the assailant's blade backwards in an attempt to get the assailant to resist and push forward. When the practitioner feels the assailant pushing back and their arm is extended the practitioner will quickly roll their elbow over the assailant's arm and pull the assailant's wrist and turn it clockwise while stepping through with the non-dominant leg. The Practitioner will also pull their blade hand to their hip. This combination of movements will effectively free the practitioner's blade hand and place the assailant in an arm bar (break the arm if required). The practitioner can now place the tip of their blade into the assailant's hand and twist until the assailant releases their blade.

## TWO LOW SEIZURE AND COUNTER SEIZURE

In this position the practitioner has attacked on the low line and the assailant has seized their wrist interrupting the practitioner's attack with their live hand. The Practitioner in turn has seized the assailant's wrist interrupting the assailant's attack. The practitioner and the assailant are in a stalemate.

## LOW STALEMATE SOLUTION ONE

The Practitioner and the assailant find themselves locked up in a two low stalemate position. The Practitioner rolls his wrist inwards over the assailant's wrist, creating a center lock / Escape. The Practitioner is now free to counter attack if necessary.

## LOW STALEMATE SOLUTION TWO

The Practitioner will take their blade hand and circle to the outside of the assailant's wrist. The Practitioner will take the butt of the blade and force downwards onto the assailant's wrist, effectively freeing their blade hand. The Practitioner should follow up immediately with a thrust or slash to the Assailant's vital target.

## LOW STALEMATE SOLUTION THREE

The Practitioner and the assailant find themselves locked up in a two low stalemate position. Practitioner pushes his hands together in a bait to have the assailant push them open. Practitioner "Shoots" under the assailant's arm towards his weapon. The Practitioner will then stand up, pulling the trapped arm across his shoulders. The Practitioner will secure the assailant's weapon hand and then is free to control or counter attack.

174

# CONFLICT ANATOMY

# &

# PHYSIOLOGY

# CONFLICT ANATOMY

## TARGETING

You should always keep in mind that the Blade is a deadly weapon and can cut through muscle and bone. It can also kill. Using the Blade is using deadly force and unless you feel your life or the life of another is in danger of GREAT BODILY HARM OR DEATH, you should not use the Blade. You may have to explain your actions in court. Some of the situations that the court may consider your actions justified include these factors:

(1) Did the individual attacking you have a weapon and what kind of weapon did he have?

(2) Did the assailant have the means and ability to cause you great bodily harm or death.

(3) Were there multiple assailants.

(4) Was there no way to escape from your assailant?

(5) Was there a way to call the police?

(6) Who started the fight?

(7) Was there no other way to avoid a physical conflict?

(8) Was there a way to handle the subject without using deadly force?

(9) Did you really feel your life was in danger?

10) Why were you carrying a Blade?

Considering that using the Blade is considered deadly force the following target areas should be considered if you have to protect your life or the life of another person.

# TYPES OF EDGED WEAPON TARGETS

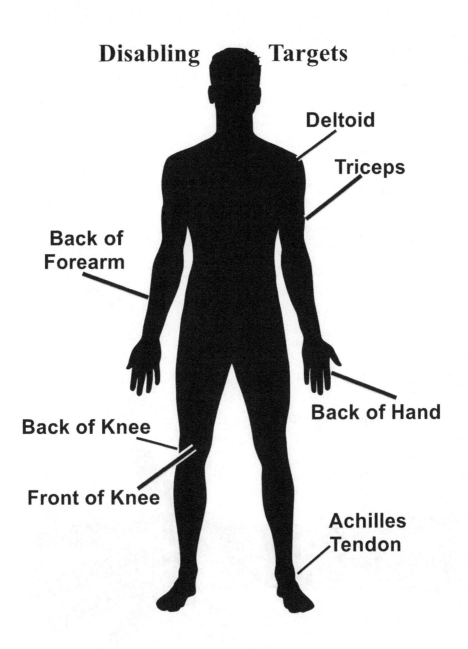

Disabling Targets

Deltoid

Triceps

Back of Forearm

Back of Hand

Back of Knee

Front of Knee

Achilles Tendon

Disabling attacks are those brought to targets that when cut or damaged are most certain to stop or seriously impair mobility or function. Like any wound a disabling attack can be lethal but is rarely so if medical attention can be acquired in a reasonable amount of time.

Targets include:

> (1) Back of the hand,
>
> (2) Back of the forearm,
>
> (3) Deltoid,
>
> (4) Triceps,
>
> (5) Front of the Knee,
>
> (6) Back of the knee/hamstring,
>
> (7) Achilles tendon

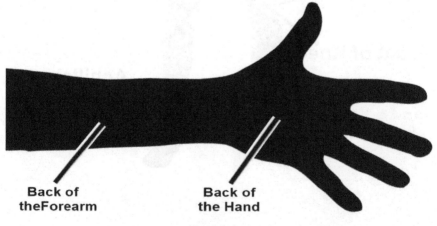

**Back of
theForearm**

**Back of
the Hand**

**Close-up of Disabling Targets 1 and 2**

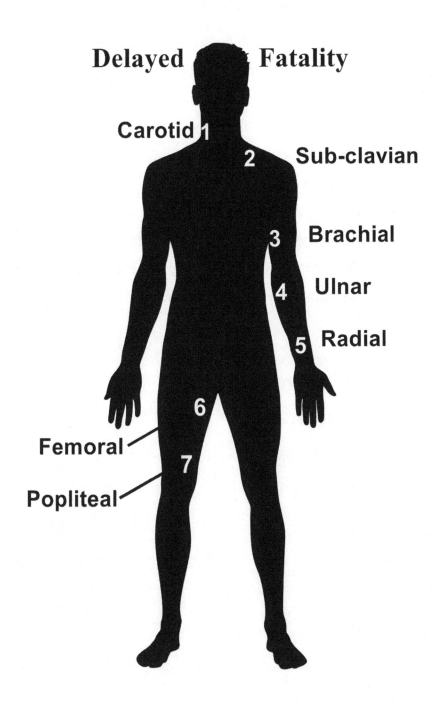

Delayed Fatality

Carotid 1

2 Sub-clavian

3 Brachial

4 Ulnar

5 Radial

6

Femoral

7

Popliteal

There are targets on the human body which when cut or damaged will result in a more or less certain fatality if not treated immediately. Without proper medical the injured individual will die due to blood loss. The injured party will likely experience light headedness, unconsciousness, and eventually die from blood loss. The rate at which impairment occurs can vary from relatively quick to relatively slow. This means that a Practitioner must be aware that even if they have received this type of wound they still have a viable chance of fighting through and controlling the situation. The survival mindset at this point is imperative for the Practitioner.

Targets include:

     (1) Carotid artery

     (2) Sub-clavian artery

     (3) Brachial artery

     (4) Ulnar artery

     (5) Radial artery

     (6) Femoral artery

     (7) Popliteal artery.

# FAST KILLS

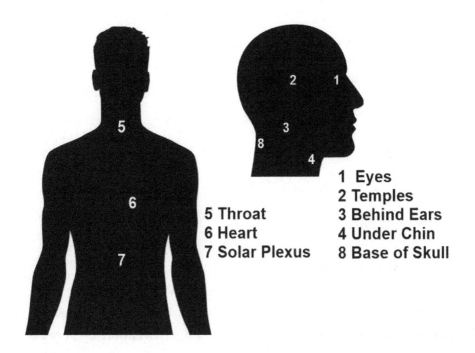

1 Eyes
2 Temples
5 Throat        3 Behind Ears
6 Heart         4 Under Chin
7 Solar Plexus  8 Base of Skull

Fast kill targets when cut or damaged will be almost immediately fatal. It is paramount that the Practitioner protect these targets areas at all times and at all costs. The sacrificing of another non-vital body part in the protection of these targets is obviously acceptable and should be employed if needed. For example, if a subject stabs at a Practitioner's eye, and the Practitioner has no option for movement, it would be acceptable for the Practitioner to cover their eye sacrificing the hand in order to avoid a fatal wound.

Targets include:

> (1) Brain via eye socket
>
> (2) Brain via temple
>
> (3) Brain via space behind the ear
>
> (4) Brain via space under the chin
>
> (5) Throat
>
> (6) Heart
>
> (7) Solar Plexus
>
> (8) Base of the Skull.

**It is crucial that Practitioners learn the edged weapon targets for two reasons:**

(1) The Practitioner can better protect themselves if they know which parts of their body are the most crucial to protect.

(2) The Practitioner can better decide appropriately as to what level of force to use since they will have a clear understanding of what their application to each body target will accomplish. Practitioner must know what targets are most likely to stop the action of the assault.

# FIGHTING WISDON

## A STICK IS NOT A BLADE

No matter how many times I tell you that it is a steak, bologna is bologna. The same holds true when it comes to stick arts vs blade arts. It is very common to hear "yes we are a blade art" but then we see the art trained with sticks.

I personally fell into this trap not knowing any better as a young martial artist. On a cursory glance the concept makes sense. When you look at it a little deeper however things do not hold up so well. The difference was driven home for me a few years back when I began working with my friend and training partner Mr. Guy Djinn. One fine morning we had planned to start working on Japanese sword together. I grabbed my favorite 36-inch wooden cane and showed up for class. My cane quickly disappeared and in its place a wooden bokken. Why? Because the bokken simulated the sword, more specifically it's edge. As the lessons progressed it became more and more evident that the nuanced lessons that I was learning with firm edge awareness could not be learned with a stick. Other things became apparent as well. The stick was lighter, the stick was evenly balanced and most importantly the stick behaved differently from steel when making contact with it's target. My light bulb turned on when I was observing a frenetic two man drills where sticks were clashing at 100MPH with full power. I looked on in awe of their stick work and realized….That is STICK work.

Is an angle one-strike the same with a stick or a blade? Sure. But combat methods are not that simple. Steel meeting steel is different than wood meeting wood. Hell, steel meeting anything is different. Once you get past the most basic techniques the stick is a blade, blade is a stick philosophy does not hold up. We must be honest and aware of this in when creating our techniques, drills and applications. Not doing so can be down right dangerous. I remember once asking Sensei Peter Brusso why he blacked a certain way with a Machete. His answer remains clear in my mind almost 15 yrs. later. "I block that way because in Vietnam, when I blocked a Machete like a stick it broke and a shard flew into my team mate's neck. That was enough of an explanation for me to take these differences seriously.

## THE WAYS OF ATTACK

When taking offensive action there are several forms that the Practitioner's offense can take. Here we seek to categorize the most common forms of attack that will be made in any engagement. A Practitioner should become familiar with all of the methods and incorporate them into their strategy and tool box. A Practitioner who only uses one or two of the methods listed here will have an incomplete offensive repertoire and will be one dimensional. This timeless breakdown comes directly from classical fencing and was adopted by Bruce Lee in his Jeet Kune Do system.

1. Progressive direct attack
2. Compound Attack or attack in combination
3. Attack by invitation
4. Progressive Indirect attack
5. Attack by Immobilization

## PROGRESSIVE DIRECT ATTACK

The Progressive direct attack is a cut or thrust that is executed in one action. In my opinion the Progressive direct attack is the sign of the novice and of the master. It is the sign of the novice because the novice has no true skill. They are one dimensional. The novice makes clumsy single simple attacks in hopes of hitting the target. The Progressive direct attack is also the sign of the master, the master who has enough skill and experience to perfectly select and time a single effective attack.

## COMPOUND ATTACK OR ATTACK IN COMBINATION

The compound attack is an attack that is executed in more than one movement. The compound attack can be a series of single attacks chained together, or a combination of feints, fakes and simple attacks. The combination of attacks can be used to overwhelm assailant if each attack has clear access to the target. In the compound attack, the initial fakes, feints or simple attacks can be used to maneuver the assailant or set up the final or primary attack in the sequence.

## ATTACK BY INVITATION

The attack by invitation is executed by adopting a posture or using a technique or feint to elicit a response from the assailant. The Practitioner is inviting an assailant to take a certain action. The Practitioner is baiting a trap. The attack by invitation is an example of using second intention strategy over first intention strategy.

## PROGRESSIVE INDIRECT ATTACK

A progressive indirect attack is an attack that begins its course in one trajectory and then changes trajectory in order to reach the target. This tactic may be done because the initial trajectory has been obstructed by the assailant's action or it may be done in order to deceive the assailant, causing them to react to one trajectory only to fall prey to another.

## ATTACK BY IMMOBILIZATION

The attack by immobilization is an attack that capitalizes on the Practitioner's ability to immobilize the assailant in some way prior to or at the same time that an attack is made. The immobilization can be completed with the live hand, the weapon, or the legs for example in a foot trap. Jamming techniques with the live hand or blade traps with the blade are the most common forms of attack.

## POINT ORIENTATION!

I watch a lot of blade players out there and I can count on one hand the ones who are truly point conscious. What do I mean by point conscious? Well it's very simple. The point of your blade should be facing the assailant at the beginning and end of every movement. I see a lot of people get in their stance and hold their blade with their tip pointing straight up. If the assailant decides to rush and press it will be easy for them because the threat is lessened by the blade pointing straight up. If you hold your blade however at a 45-degree angle pointing at the assailant, there is a threat for him to get past. Even in the event that the Practitioner is not consciously defending and the assailant rushes there is a good chance that they will impale themselves on the Practitioner's blade.

When making cuts most people's blade point will be facing in the direction in which they cut. Rather than doing this, when the Practitioner cuts they should be forever conscious of ensuring that their blade point is facing the assailant at the end of their movement. By being point conscious the Practitioner helps his defense by always returning to a protected position rather than exposing themselves to bad posture. The Practitioner after every attack should find themselves back in one of the nine wards with their point directed at their assailant. Being point conscious will require a tiny modification of your body mechanics but trust me it will become second nature and is in your best interests.

## OF TIME AND MEASURE & RHYTHM

To the reader, please take note. While other sections of this book are important, I strongly believe that aside from strong fundamentals, the three concepts discussed here are arguably the most important topics within this book. The space dedicated to them is relatively brief when compared to other topics in the book but do not be fooled. Without a good understanding of these topics a student will never develop or attain any real measure of skill. An understanding of distance, time and rhythm is the one common thread which I have found amongst all of those who I would consider having true skill regardless of the system they study. The ability to truly understand Time, Measure and Rhythm can only come from mindful free play, sparring or similar drills. With enough practice the Practitioner will begin to internalize these concepts and develop an instinctive ability to apply them correctly for both offense and defense.


## TEMPO

The term Tempo is used differently by different authors and coaches. The two primary ways to define Tempo that we will use are as follow and will be referred to as Tempo A and Tempo B:

1. Tempo refers to an opportune moment to strike at the assailant.
2. Tempo refers to the time that it takes to complete any one action while within measure of the assailant.

In "Great Representation of the Art and Use of Fencing", Ridolfo Capo Ferro of Cagli instructs several circumstances when it is an ideal time to strike the assailant. Those times are:

- When the assailant is fixed in guard and lifts or moves his lead foot
- When you have parried a blow
- When he moves himself carelessly from one guard to another
- When the assailant's attack has travelled past your body
- When the assailant raises his weapon

It is important to think of the Tempo as a "moment of opportunity". Tempo is the precise and correct moment in which to launch your attack. While the Practitioner will inevitably find other moments of opportunity, the list provided to us by Capo Ferro is very useful in helping the Practitioner begin to identify these tempos. The Practitioner should remember that while they can become adept at reading their assailant and identifying tempos, they may also become adept at creating tempos through craftiness and invitation. My Silat instructor the late Eddie Ivester was fond of saying, "Other systems look for openings, we create openings".

Fencing instructor Tommaso Leoni in his article *"Understanding Tempo"* explains that Fencing Master Fabris established a theoretical rule as to how a Practitioner will identify that opportune moment to act against the assailant. Master Leoni explains that *"Fabris states that you should take a tempo if the time required for your offense is*

191

*less or equal to that required for the opponent's defense. ""The reason why Fabris says less or equal (instead of just less) is that you have the advantage of having moved first."*

## STESSO TEMPO.

Stesso Tempo refers to single time. In Stesso tempo, the Practitioner's defense and counter attack happen at the same time. The defensive-counterattacking response is performed in a "single time", or "stesso tempo" in Italian: the attacking move, and the responding defense and counter-attack occur at the same time. Stesso tempo is also referred to as "Parallel motion"

## DUI TEMPO.

Dui Tempi translates as two times. This term refers to when there are two separate and consecutive movements. A classic example of Dui Tempi is a parry and riposte. Dui tempo is also referred to as "Serial Motion".

## MEZZO TEMPO.

Mezzo tempo refers to "in the middle", as in the middle of the assailant's movement. When the assailant is beginning a movement, let's say a change in the position of the weapon hand the Practitioner can launch their attack "In the middle" of their assailant's movement and make contact.

## CONTRA TEMPO

Contra Tempo or Counter Time has varying definitions depending on the source. For our purpose we will define Counter Time as when the Practitioner makes an intentional movement (tempo) in order to prompt or provoke the assailant to attack, at which time the Practitioner will exploit their provocation and counter that attack.

## TRUE TIME

Smooth is fast. Fast is NOT smooth. Do you see my point? Let me explain in case you don't. The other day a friend of mine sent me a video clip. The clip was of two people blade sparring. The people in the video come from a pretty well known "Blade Camp." I watched it and jokingly replied to my friend by asking if it was an instructional video on how to telegraph your movements. You see in the video the two combatants were fast, and I mean FAST. They both obviously had really trained their natural attributes to a high level. The problem was that even though they were ridiculously fast they both telegraphed their movement terribly. The people I watched in the video were very fast, but they were not very smooth. Speed of technique comes from smoothness of technique and smoothness of technique comes from proper repetition of proper body mechanics. Their great physical speed is most likely enough to compensate for this against the average student but anyone with any advanced training would probably take them apart fairly easily. It is a shame really because with their natural gift of speed as an attribute all they would need is to learn to be a little smoother with their motions and they would be phenomenal fighters.

Telegraphing movement is a problem, it is an ailment for which we do have the prescription. So, what is the prescription for this ailment and where do we find it? Well the answer is this. The prescription for the lack of smooth, non-telegraphed movement is "True Time" and we find it in the works of Englishman George Silver.

**George Silver** was an English man who lived during the late 16th and early 17th century. Silver was an advocate of the English backsword and often portrayed as xenophobic. In reality Silver was simply a proud English man who believed in the English traditions. His criticisms of the Foreign Rapier methods in vogue in England in his time are actually well thought out and well supported arguments. I learned along time ago that you should never criticize a method unless you are prepared to offer a better solution and have the ability to support your position. Silver arguably does this in his criticism of the rapier and the methods of its instruction. Silver wrote two important works on swordsmanship; *Paradoxes of Defence and Brief Instructions on my Paradoxes of Defence.* Both manuals have proven influential to this day. The later was used to help train soldiers fighting in the Boer War.

In Paradoxes of Defense, Silver tells us: "There are eight times, whereof four are true, and four are false. "

| TRUE TIMES | FALSE TIMES |
|---|---|
| The time of the hand. | The time of the foot. |
| The time of the hand and body. | The time of the foot and body. |
| The time of the hand, body, and foot. | The time of the foot, body, and hand. |
| The time of the hand, body, and feet. | The time of the feet, body, and hand. |

*"Thus, have I thought good to separate and make known the true times from the false, with the true wards thereto belonging, that thereby the rather in practicing of weapons a true course may be taken for the avoiding of errors and evil customs, and speedy attaining of good habit or perfect being in the true use and knowledge of all manner of weapons." –George Silver*

When using the True Times, we move in such a way that allows for two important things. Those two things are non-telegraphic movement and the most protected postures possible. If you take a look at the false times you see why using false time will telegraph your movements. Silver wisely advises us to follow the movement progression of Hand-Body-Foot/Feet. By moving in this progression our movements will be smooth and non-telegraphic. Think of a sparring match. If your opponent leads with their foot or their body, it is almost certain that you will be able detect their intention and easily respond. By moving in the proper progression laid out in the true times we are much less likely to telegraph our movements. The hand moves faster than the body or the feet. If the hand is moving first, it is less detectable than say leaning your body in first or taking a big step. This is why weapon to the rear stances in dueling situations are virtual suicide. Leading with the hand and therefore the weapon also provides us more protection. The weapon is out in front, able to attack or defend quickly. The hand moves quickly. If a Practitioner extends their hand and then realizes that the assailant is able to counter, the Practitioner will have a decent chance of compensating. If a Practitioner is leading with their feet or body, then they will be hard pressed to compensate for an assailant's counter. There will simply not be enough time. Hema and modern tactical blade instructor Keith Jennings offers these additional insights;

*The "hand" is really the weapon. A lot of people criticize true times because they think you are leading with your hand, which will get cut in sword/blade fight. In reality it is weapon first. As long as the weapon enters range first, then you are moving in a true time. The Weapon moving first also presents a threat that our opponent cannot ignore. By moving with the weapon first the opponent is forced to defend instead of just launching their own attack."*

Most modern schools that I have sampled make no mention at all of what Silver calls the true times or any similar concept. Some schools teach that the hand and body/foot must move simultaneously. This is a better approach than ignoring the true times all together and in my experience this approach can be functional when working with smaller blades. Silver's explanation of true and false time however is hands down the best explanation of the concept that I have found. I highly recommend that the Practitioner embrace the concept. We may not all be naturally fast, but we can all learn to move in a smarter fashion.

## OF MEASURE

Measure is distance. It is crucial that the Practitioner learn and fully understand the concepts of measure. No useful attack or defense can be successfully completed without factoring in the correct measure. I have watched countless sparring sessions with men who possess both ample training and the titles to go with and It never ceases to amaze me how poorly they handle the issue of proper distance. Their attacks fail because they lack knowledge of the proper measure needed to attack and their defense fails because they understand the measure needed for defense even less. In my opinion, no art can compare to the Western sword arts when it comes to understanding and properly applying principles of measure. When attempting to understand measure, I refer to two sources which have given us two different but equally functional ways to approach the subject.

Alfred Hutton was a Victorian era English officer of the King's Dragoon Guards, and Fencing instructor. Hutton was trained in the methods of the Italian swordsmen from an early age and expanded his studies to the English backsword, bayonet and other weapons. Hutton was an advocate of both military and historical fencing. Hutton wrote several books on fencing with both the sword and bayonet. In his work "COLD STEEL" Alfred Hutton explained the following regarding distance and measure;

*Distance or measure is the exact space, taken in a straight line between the combatants, which must be traversed by the lunge.*

*Perfect Measure* is when on the lunge, and without having previously moved the left foot, you can strike some part of the opponent.

*Out of Measure* is when it is necessary to advance at least one step in order to be near enough to touch the adversary.

*Within Measure* is when you are so near that you can touch or be touched without lunging.

*Corp d Corps* is when the combatants have come so close together that it is possible for them to grapple with each other.

Professor Steven J. Pearlman in his book, *"The Book of Martial Power"* sums it up nicely when he states that "Positioning dictates a singular place to locate ourselves during combat: where we can affect the opponent and where the opponent cannot affect us".

Being in measure should be a decision that the Practitioner makes. The Practitioner who finds themselves within measure because of the assailant's actions has been put at a disadvantage. In "Fencing: Ancient Art & Modern Sport", C.L. de Beaumont states that "Variations of measure will make it more difficult for the opponent to time his attacks or preparations." Remember that by controlling measure the Practitioner can control the encounter.

## PROXIMITY NEGATES SKILL

Many of my teachers have advocated an approach to blade work that attempts to avoid the close-range game. Others advocate being eye to eye with an assailant. I understand that these opposing view points often come from the nature of the systems that produce them. Civilian instructors seem to be much more concerned with range. Military instructors that I have worked with work efficiently on closing the gap and taking it to the assailant. On this subject I feel that Modern Master at Arms Lynn Thompson has the soundest advice. Mr. Thompson in the article **"20 Essentials You Need to Know About Using and Defending Against Cold Steel"** was quoted as saying *"If you can get five or 10 feet away from your adversary quickly and you're the one with the skill, you will have an enormous advantage over him." "You can debilitate him without allowing him a chance to retaliate. He will be in a vulnerable position and he won't even realize it. "But if you insist on fighting toe-to-toe and he has the motivation, he will have an excellent chance of maiming or killing you, too," he says. "Remember that the closer your adversary is to you, the less your skill counts." A good blade fighter knows how to fight at close range, but he doesn't like it because he knows proximity gives advantages to even an unskilled opponent, Thompson says. "It's not good to be in a position where he can touch you without even moving. He doesn't need to have power to win; all he needs is the will."*

## RHYTHM

Rhythm refers to a pattern of movements that are repeated continuously during the course of an encounter. A Practitioner will inevitably find themselves in a rhythm when attacking, defending, and moving in general. Rhythm can be very useful to a Practitioner in gaining or maintaining momentum during an encounter, but the Practitioner must know when to break rhythm or alter it. The reason for this is that with enough time an astute assailant will be able to read the Practitioner's rhythm and intercept with their attack. Inversely, a Practitioner can use rhythm as a ruse, as a form of attack by invitation. A Practitioner should always seek to set the rhythm of the engagement. Fight the fight on your own terms, not the assailant's.

The Practitioner should learn two important keys to rhythm. Those keys are:
  1. Defensive use of breaking a rhythm
  2. Offensive use of Variable Acceleration

## BREAKING A RHYTHM

In sparring I have found myself "feeling" threatened by my opponent. When I took the time to analyze why I felt this way I realized that I was feeling threatened because I was falling prey to my opponent's rhythm. My opponent had established a positive rhythm and was gaining an advantageous momentum. My reactions themselves were becoming part of the overall rhythm of the engagement. I found that in order to protect myself I needed to break the assailant's rhythm.

This can be accomplished in a variety of ways. The simplest is to simply retreat from measure. By removing yourself from the equation the rhythm can no longer exist. Another method of breaking the rhythm is to alter your reactions and movements. Often the assailant is able to establish a positive rhythm that benefits them because our actions and reactions play into their game. STOP! and be mindful of your contributions to the overall rhythm of the fight. A 180 degree turn (figuratively) in your motions may just be what is needed to break the assailant's positive rhythm.

## VARIABLE ACCELERATION

Movements in a fight have a certain measurable speed. Just like beats in music, martial motions can be completed in full beats, half beats, quarter beats, etc. When exchanging with an assailant, the assailant will grow accustomed to our speed. This recognition of the Practitioner's speed gives the assailant a fair chance of executing a defense before the Practitioner's attack can be completed. If the Practitioner however alters their acceleration from fast to slow or slow to fast, the assailant can be fooled. The assailant expects a certain velocity. When faced with a different one than what they expected they must mentally process the change and often can be fooled. In his book, "The Book of Martial Power", Professor Steven J. Pearlman states that *"Operating outside the normal beat structure will do wonders to disrupt our opponent's timing, positioning and angling."* I have done this many times in sparring. I will initiate 2 or 3 very rapid cuts to establish with my assailant that I am coming hard and fast. I then casually extend my blade out and reach my target with no interference. Usually the assailant is watching me the entire time. I can see in their eyes that they are recognizing this change in acceleration, but they often are too far behind the curve to make a good defense possible.

# FIGHT LIKE THE RAVEN

If you watch a Raven in the wild you will see the tactic. When a raven approaches a carcass that it has identified as food it never goes directly to the body. It is actually somewhat comical to watch. The Raven will begin by stepping forward close to the carcass and then jumps back away from the body. The Raven may do this once or twice more and when the Raven is convinced that the body is in fact dead and only then will the Raven move in. In blade combat I was taught to apply the same tactic as the Raven. We must keep in mind that while blade combat can resemble a trip to hell, at times it also resembles a good game of chess. A thinking Practitioner will use the Raven tactic to learn something about their assailant, something that can be used against them. A simple example of the Raven tactic in play is as follows:


The Practitioner and the assailant face off. The Practitioner will make a weak attack at say the assailant's hand. The assailant reacts by pulling his hand to the right. The Practitioner sees this and makes note. The Practitioner then continues along with his action, and a little later the Practitioner will make the same weak attack at the assailant's hand and allows the assailant time to react. The assailant reacts by pulling his hand to the right. Again, the Practitioner knows this. The Practitioner then continues along with his action, and a little later the Practitioner will make the same attack once again. This time when the assailant pulls his hand to the right the Practitioner, knowing his path will be clear, alters his attack and thrusts directly into the assailant's unprotected chest. In this manner the Practitioner fought like the Raven and gained knowledge of his assailant before committing to an attack. The Raven is wise. If the assailant had reacted differently each time to the Practitioner's weak attacks, then the Practitioner would have learned that the assailant's actions would not be easy to predict and would have moved on to another strategy. In this case however the Practitioner fought like a Raven and was able to finish the assailant.

## THE FOUR GOVERNORS

George Silver in his works discussed why trained men were often hurt or killed by men of little or no training. His exact words were: *"many valiant men think themselves by their practices to be skillful in their weapons, are yet many times in their fights sore hurt, and many times slain by men of small skill or none at all."*

Silver identified above all other causes the lack of the Four Governors was to blame for this condition. Silver expressed that without the Four Governors it is impossible to fight safely. When reviewing the Four Governors you will see that they are points of very sound advice and should be taken to heart by any Practitioner who is serious about their study of arms. The Four Governors serve as a guideline and foundation for success in combat. Let us introduce you to the Governors as described in Silver's work "BRIEF INSTRUCTIONS UPON MY PARADOXES OF DEFENCE".

*"The first governor is judgment which is to know when your adversary can reach you, and when not, and when you can do the like to him, and to know by the goodness or badness of his lying, what he can do, and when and how he can perform it."*

Judgment can be said to be the Practitioner's ability to analyze their assailant and the overall factors of the engagement. Judgment is insight and the ability to recognize factors crucial to gaining victory. Silver makes it very clear that Judgment will allow us to understand the distance of attack and defense. Judgment will also give us an understanding of what the assailant is capable of.

*"The second governor is measure. Measure is the better to know how to make your space true to defend yourself, or to offend your enemy."*

Measure is one of the most crucial lessons a Practitioner can learn. Without proper measure which includes a firm understanding of range and timing, all other training would surely fail.

*"The third and forth governors are a twofold mind when you press in on your enemy, for as you have a mind to go forward, so must you have at that instant a mind to fly backward upon any action that shall be offered or done by your adversary."*

The third and forth Governors relate the importance of being ready to seize the opportunity to attack as well as to being able to recognize the moment to retreat.

An understanding of Silver's Governors will improve the practitioner's ability to fight safely.

## BALANCE

Physical balance refers to the body's ability to be in proper structure at all times. Proper structure will allow the Practitioner to move, defend and attack from a position of stability. By studying the proper techniques of footwork, defense and offense the Practitioner will ensure that they are maximizing the benefits of proper body structure and skeletal alignment. Even the slightest deficit to correct structure can cause catastrophic consequences. Remember that an edged weapon encounter is not the type of situation that allows a person to make too many errors. One can very well be one too many. In the assailant, the Practitioner should seek to exploit weaknesses identified in the assailant's balance and even proactively force the assailant into poor balance. If the assailant is unable to find their physical balance they will be easier to defeat.

In addition to physical balance the Practitioner must seek mental balance. There is an old saying that "Most fights are won or lost in the mind". A Practitioner who is unable to remain focused and calm will be weak. Concepts such as conflict rehearsal, survival stress management and Mushin are all explained in this work and should be mastered by the Practitioner. When confronting an assailant, the Practitioner should seek to mentally unbalance them. Intimidation, distraction, and deception can be used to this end.

## SPEED

Fluid motion is a source of speed. Repetitious training of proper angles of attack and defense, footwork and technique provide the Practitioner a certain fluidity of motion. Even a "Slow" person can become fast when they have acquired a high level of familiarity with the lines of attack and defense. I like to use the example of typing to illustrate this type of speed. In typing class, I would hunt and peck for letters. It would take me about 10 minutes to type a few sentences. With time and practice I now easily type close to 70 words a minute without looking at the key board, without hesitating. I am able to just flow on the keys with speed. It is the same for the skills of the Practitioner. Proper practice will lead to proper form and then proper speed. The USMC saying is true, "Slow is smooth, and smooth is FAST." Our other source for speed is a gift from God. Fast twitch muscle fibers in the body provide natural speed. The kind of speed found in gifted athletes. This type of speed can be developed slightly but by in large it is a set attribute.

## MOMENTUM

Physical momentum refers to the body's ability to stay in motion. For the Practitioner this means that they will seek to flow from one position to another seeking increased advantage in each movement. The series of movements will culminate with the defeat of the assailant. The assailant through their defense will seek to break the momentum of the Practitioner. Mental Momentum refers to the minds ability to see the logical chains of progression of physical movements to an advantageous outcome. The Practitioner must be able to visualize their movement, successfully following it through to the next and so on.

## DON'T BE IN SUCH A RUSH TO DIE!

I have had the good fortune of traveling around the world to teach Blade work to students from all walks of life. In my seminars I often ask the participants to take a moment and think about who they consider to be the most dangerous person in the world with a blade. Inevitably responses come back such as Dan Inosanto, Nene Tortal, or some black bag spec ops type. Then tell them that I will bet them my pay check that I could kill any of the names on their list with a blade. This is about the point where I hear dissatisfied sighs and start seeing eye balls rolling. This is the point where I get the looks that say "Vargas, you are not half bad but dam! You're an arrogant son of a bitch". Once I have acquired the disdain of the crowd then explain to them an important lesson. I explain that killing someone with a blade is not that hard. Not hard if you have no concern for your own safety. I do believe that if I made a one-shot kamikaze run with a blade I could kill virtually any opponent out there. The problem with that is that more times than not I would-be dead-on arrival as well. " Don't be in such a rush to die". Rushing in on a blade wielding adversary is courting death. I like to share with students what I call a "Light Bulb Phrase". I call it that because whenever I speak it I can literally see light bulbs going off over student's heads. This very important phrase is "There is a difference between killing the other guy and not getting killed". Once I communicate this idea I always see a radical change in the students when they spar. Before sharing it with them they looked like rocke'em sock'em robots. Always in measure trading shots, like two guys stuck in a blender. After sharing the idea however I start to see some thought going on. Students start to pick their shots; they focus on maintaining a good defense and are a whole lot more concerned with staying alive. Now while I will concede that there are some individuals in high risk professions who may need to keep the goal of "Kill the other guy" by in large most civilians and even law enforcement personnel will be much better served by the "Don't get killed" mind set. So, use your head, mount a strong defense, use a calculated offense not a kamikaze one, focus on staying alive and most importantly "DON'T BE IN SUCH A RUSH TO DIE."

# BLIOGRAPHY

1. TRADIZIONI SCHERMISTICHE IN LIGURIA E PIEMONTE BY GILBERTO PAUCIULLO & ANTONIO GG MERENDONI
2. INFANTRY SWORD EXERCISE BY HENRY CHARLES ANGELO
3. BROAD SWORD FIGHTING BY PAUL PORTER
4. TREATISE ON FENCING BY MICHAL STARZEWSKI.
5. TEATRO BY NICOLETTO GIGANTI
6. FIGHTING WITH THE SABER BY NORMAN J. FINKELSHTEYN
7. INTRODUCTION TO ITALIAN RAPIER BY DAVID AND DORI COBLENTZ
8. THE ART AND THE SCIENCE, AN INTRODUCTION TO RAPIER TECHNIQUES OF SALVATOR FABRIS BY PHIL MARSHALL
9. PATH OF THE RONIN BY KEVIN SECOURS
10. RENAISSANCE RAPIER TECHNIQUE AND TACTICS BY JOSEPH "BLAYDE" BRICKY
11. OLD SWORD PLAY BY ALFRED HUTTON
12. HONOR, MASCULINITY, AND RITUAL BLADE FIGHTING IN NINETEENTH-CENTURY GREECE BY THOMAS GALLANT
13. GREAT REPRESENTATION OF THE ART AND USE OF FENCING BY RIDOLFO CAPO FERRO OF CAGLI
14. FENCING BY WALTER H. POLLOCK, F.C. GROVE & CAMILLE PREVOST.
15. EVOLUTION OF THE USMC BIDDLE METHOD BY DANIEL TREMBULA
16. MILITARY GEOLOGY AND THE APACHE WARS, SOUTH WEST UNITED STATES BY PETER DOYLE
17. THE APACHES: AMERICA'S GREATEST GUERILLA FIGHTERS BY BLAISE LOONG
18. SLASH & THRUST BY JOHN SANCHEZ
19. BLADE MASTER BY JOHN SANCHEZ
20. MONADNOCK DEFENSIVE TACTICS SYSTEM MANUAL JOSEPH TRUNCALE & TERRY E. SMITH
21. STUDENT FENCING GUIDE BY ALFRED LOUIE
22. COLD STEEL BY ALFRED HUTTON
23. ESSENTIALS OF FENCING TECHNIQUE BY RICHARD HOWARD
24. HAND WORK FOR DUELING BY LARRY TOM
25. INTRODUCTION TO THE MEDIEVAL LONG SWORD BY THE CHICAGO SWORD PLAY GUILD
26. DAGA, BY CHRISTOPHER PENNEY & NICHOLAS CONWAY
27. THE ANNOTATED FABRIS BY KRISTOPHE SPRENGER
28. TRATTO DI SCIENZIA D'ARMES, BY CAMILLO AGRIPPA
29. THE ART OF COMBAT BY JOACHIM MEYER

30. GREAT REPRESENTATION OF THE ART AND USE OF FENCING BY RIDOLFO CAPO FERRO
31. UNDERSTANDING TEMPO BY TOMMASO LEONI
32. SEVILLIAN STEEL BY JAMES LORIEGA
33. PARADOXES OF DEFENCE BY GEORGE SILVER
34. BRIEF INSTRUCTIONS ON MY PARADOXES OF DEFENCE BY GEORGE SILVER
35. COLD STEEL BY ALFRED HUTTON
36. THE BOOK OF MARTIAL POWER BY PROFESSOR STEVEN J. PEARLMAN
37. 20 ESSENTIALS YOU NEED TO KNOW ABOUT USING AND DEFENDING AGAINST COLD STEEL BY LYNN THOMPSON
38. THE TRUE MEANING OF JU IN JUDO AND JUJITSU BY ANDREW VIANNAKIS PHD AND LINDA VIANNAKIS M.S.
39. THE SCHOOL OF FENCING BY MR. ANGELO
40. ARCHERY, FENCING, AND BROADSWORD BY "STONEHENGE," AND THE REV. J. G. WOOD.
41. MILITARY BLADE FIGHTING BY ROBERT K. SPEAR
42. RAPIER FUNDAMENTALS BY DARREN DI BATTISTA
43. EPEE TEMPO BY COACH ALLEN EVANS
44. THE SECOND INTENTION TACTIC IN GERMAN FECHBUCH OF 16TH CENTURY BY GEORGE E. GEORGAS

# ABOUT THE AUTHOR

Mr. Vargas is a lifelong martial artist who has dedicated a significant portion of his career to the study of edged weapons. He is recognized as an edged weapon subject matter expert; Mr. Vargas holds instructor rankings in several edged weapons curriculums ranging from Native American blade combatives, Kali, Kenjutsu, Guazabara Machete Fencing and several others. He is the only American to be granted the title of *Soma de Cutel* by Grand Master Gilberto Pauciullo and the Instituto per le Tradisioni Marziali Italiane. Mr. Vargas has also been awarded the honorific title of *Master Blade Instructor* by his Sifu David Seiwert and the designation of *Master at Arms* by Ernest Emerson and the Order of the Black Shamrock. As an author Mr. Vargas has written over a dozen books on the subject of edged weapons.

As a certified Law Enforcement Defensive Tactics Instructor, Mr. Vargas has taught edged weapons and counter edged weapon tactics to law enforcement officers at the local, state, and federal level, as well as security officers, military personnel and private citizens from around the United States and foreign nations such as Canada, Italy, and Spain. Mr. Vargas has developed programs which have been approved by the Police officer training and Standards Board of several states and adopted by agencies such as the Pentagon Force protection Agency. Additionally, organizations such as the Fraternal Order of Law Enforcement and the International Academy of Executive Protection Agents have given formal endorsements of the programs developed by Mr. Vargas and Raven Tactical International. Mr. Vargas has been a multi time instructor at the prestigious International Law Enforcement Educators & Trainers Association International Conference (ILEETA).

**www.TheRavenTribe.com**

**www.RavenTactical.com**

**www.RavenTalkPodcast.com**

The "Combat Machete Volume One" written by good friend and student Fernan Vargas, has presented one of the most simple, no frills, and relatively easy to learn approaches to combat machete out there today.

The book provides an excellent explanation on how to use the combat blade for self-defense. The clear descriptions of the use and techniques are simple with well placed photos and diagrams. The historical pieces are just enough to highlight points concerning its use in war, Asia, South America and the streets. Not overbearing.

The combat principals and legal aspects of force explained in this book were very clear. It helps one to adopt a more realistic approach to training in self-defense for civilian individuals. It is guide to developing a combat mindset that will allow you to effectively avoid confrontation, and put your combat skills to use effectively when retreat is not an option.

Simple and straight forward, this book and the author's message is excellent in its presentation. It is not complicated, but a clear and concise formula for any individual in today's age who is confronted with such situations can defend themselves.

This book epitomizes its subject matter right down to the bare bones of reality-lean, valid, relevant and practical, with nothing extra.

Miguel Quijano
El Juego De Mani
Student of the late Juan De Dios
Cocobale